Beyond Christianity

Beyond Christianity

African Americans in a New Thought Church

Darnise C. Martin

New York University Press

NEW YORK AND LONDON

NEW YORK UNIVERSITY PRESS
New York and London
www.nyupress.org

Library of Congress Cataloging-in-Publication Data
Martin, Darnise C.
Beyond Christianity : African Americans in a
New Thought church / Darnise C. Martin.
p. cm. — (Religion, race, and ethnicity)
Includes bibliographical references (p.) and index.
ISBN 0–8147–5693–X (cloth : alk. paper)
1. East Bay Church of Religious Science (Oakland, Calif.)
2. African Americans—California—Oakland—Religion.
I. Title. II. Series.
BP605.U53M37   2005
299'.93—dc22   2004019292

New York University Press books are printed on acid-free paper,
and their binding materials are chosen for strength and durability.

Manufactured in the United States of America

c 10 9 8 7 6 5 4 3 2 1
p 10 9 8 7 6 5 4 3 2 1

For my mother, Catherine, who always set the bar high;
my grandmother Jessie, who allowed me to just be;
my two fathers;
and all my uncles, aunts, and cousins
who make up a family

Contents

Acknowledgments

I thank my family, friends, and colleagues, who have lent support in more ways than I can list. I also thank the teachers and professors who encouraged me along the way.

I thank my editor, Jennifer Hammer, whose foresight brought this book to fruition.

I also acknowledge the ancestors upon whose shoulders I now stand.

Introduction

The predominately African American congregation fills three services at the East Bay Church of Religious Science (EBCRS) on Sunday mornings. Members and visitors come regularly to this church in downtown Oakland, California, that is known throughout the community for its lively, uplifting environment, accomplished gospel choir, and empowering sermons that teach a philosophy called Religious Science. The East Bay Church of Religious Science sustains a community that successfully embodies an African American worship environment while simultaneously modeling the tenets of a historically White New Thought religion. To date there is not much known about those African Americans who take part in this religion. This book, the first to focus on African American religious scientists, is a start toward filling that niche.

This work is significant because the attraction of the East Bay Church of Religious Science to African Americans has considerable ramifications for the way the concept of "African American religion" is defined and discussed. I lift up Religious Science as a type of religious modality that has largely been overlooked in the African American religious studies literature. The study of the EBCRS expands our scholarly conversations beyond the historical focus upon Christianity and Islam as legitimate religious practices in which African American people are engaged. This

book advances the religious pluralism discourse by inviting
the voices of Religious Science and New Thought generally
to the mainstream discussion of American religions.

Background and Approach

Religious Science, or Science of Mind as it is also called, is a
religious and philosophical teaching that was developed by
Ernest Holmes in 1927. It is built upon a pantheistic system
of universal and spiritual principles and the practical application of these principles to one's life. African Americans involved in Religious Science represent an exception
to traditional descriptions of African American religious
practices. While there are a handful of established and
prominent African American New Thought churches
around the United States such as The Universal Foundation For Better Living in Chicago, Hillside Chapel and
Truth Center in Atlanta, and Agape International Center of
Truth in Los Angeles, there has been no research on the
phenomenon of African Americans who belong to and regularly participate in these movements. This book seeks to
respond to this void through an ethnographic study of the
East Bay Church of Religious Science (EBCRS) in Oakland,
California. My work with the EBCRS community offers
original research and insight into the intersection of Religious Science and African American cultural aesthetics as
observed within the context of a particular Oakland congregation. I present an original ethnography that illustrates
the beliefs, values, and worship practices of East Bay
Church of Religious Science. Through data gathered as a
participant-observer, I have determined that it is the *intersection* of New Thought doctrine, characterized by personal empowerment and abundance teachings, and a cul-

turally familiar liturgical style reminiscent of the music, preaching style and congregational responses of Black Pentecostals and Black Spiritualists, that has lead to the success of this church.

Because terms like "culture" and "aesthetics" are somewhat slippery and raise a host of complex questions themselves, I narrow my analysis in this work to a model of African American cultural aesthetics that is informed by shared historical memories, religious aspects of performed culture, and a cultural politics of difference that allows for legitimate intra-cultural variation. This ethnography has the potential to be a valuable resource on this underrepresented denomination and for an underrepresented population within it.

The ethnographic method has allowed me to sort out any aesthetic distinctions that African Americans in this congregation may bring to Religious Science. By participating in the worship services at EBCRS, I have been able to view and experience the intersection of aesthetic and philosophy that leads African American participants to embrace this church. I have witnessed the mixture of Science of Mind philosophy/theology with the particular form of African American spirituality delivered through the lived experiences of a minister steeped in southern folk wisdom and a Pentecostal background that creates the unique atmosphere at this church. Here, Religious Science is taught in a context aesthetically familiar to its African American participants.

I conducted the majority of the field work over a period of nearly two years, from June 2001 into early 2003. This included regular attendance at Sunday services for that time as well as some Wednesday night healing services and participation in Religious Science Foundations Class for four months at the end of 2000. Since the church began the process of moving to a new location in May of 2002, a significant event in the life of the church began to occur near the end of my field work period. Therefore, my descriptions and conclusions will be drawn mostly on the experiences of the previous location, and to a lesser degree on the transitional period of moving and full residence in the new facility.

For the purpose of clarity I offer a few procedural remarks. First, I must acknowledge that I have been attending the East Bay Church of Religious Science for the past six years as my primary place of worship. While I did not begin attending the church with research in mind, I now find myself writing about it. Through the historian of religions, Charles Long, I became interested in ideas of cultural contact and exchange, and I wanted to pursue those ideas alongside the ways in which people construct and reconstruct existential meaning through religion. I eventually realized that my own congregation was a model of a cultural group which has reconstructed their religious identities in a nontraditional way. Since this congregation is part of my own spiritual practice I acknowledge, in advance, the complexities that are present in the project. However, I also recognize that my position as a participant at this church does not prohibit scholarly research. I acknowledge with history of religions scholar Joachim Wach that being a member of the faith tradition which one is studying need not be a prejudicial disadvantage, but can be a favorable precondition.[1] However, I seek to inform my readers of my social location, and remain mindful of my own biases as is necessary for any researcher whether the community in question is known or unknown.

The names of all interview participants are pseudonyms (except for the minister) for the protection of their privacy.

The vernacular of EBCRS requires that I make a distinction between the capitalized term "Practitioner" and my own nonspecific use of lower case "practitioner." The former refers to the professional title of the lay leaders within the church, and the latter I use, more generally, to refer to people who ascribe to this religious tradition. All biblical scripture references correspond to the New Revised Standard Version (NRSV).

Chapter 1 will necessarily include a historical overview of Religious Science and its origins out of the larger New Thought movement. I explore the religious and philosophical teachings of New Thought within the context of nineteenth-century New England, and follow the development of those ideas as they became expressed in the form of Religious Science.

In chapter 2, I cover a vast period of American history. I begin with the social and religious location of Africans in the New World, and the extent to which African retentions might have influenced the religious behaviors of African Americans. I then move forward in time to discuss African American religious behaviors of the twentieth century, particularly in light of the social effects of the northern migration of many Blacks from the South. This section focuses upon exploring the affinities between New Thought religious ideals, Black Spiritualism, and Black Pentecostalism. Additionally, I present some contemporary African American Christian ministers who are incorporating New Thought teachings into their sermons. They represent the phenomenon of contemporary Black megachurches, where memberships often soar in the range of 5,000 to 20,000 plus congregants. Their inclusion of New Thought principles speaks to the syncretism that is characteristic of many African American churches, regardless of their denomination. The chapter will help to situate the East Bay Church of Religious Science within a historical syncretism of African American religious expressions.

In chapter 3, I explore the historical and religious milieu of the San Francisco Bay Area, touching upon the larger context of California's religious history. The chapter presents some of the experiences of African American early settlers and the later World War II migrants. I discuss the idea of new religious sensibilities that were given voice in California, distinct from the more conservative, old world sensibility of the east and the fundamentalism of the southern states. Some of the members of East Bay Church of Religious Science describe how their sensibilities inform their decisions to attend the church.

In chapter 4, I present my findings and draw conclusions based upon interviews conducted with twenty members of East Bay Church of Religious Science, and based upon my experiences as a participant-observer over a roughly two-year period. I begin to fill in the congregational picture by adding more detail about particular members and describing church activities as a whole. Using the methods of ethnography and phenomenology I begin to analyze my findings.

Reflecting the ethnographic task as spelled out by anthropologist James Spradley, who wrote that "the purpose of ethnography is to describe and explain the regularities and variations in social behavior,"[2] I seek to describe a variation of African American religious practices in order to contrast it with the standard monolithic discussion of African American religious life. I affirm with Spradley that, "ethnography allows us to see alternative realities and modify our culture bound theories of human behavior."[3] My engagement with the East Bay Church of Religious Science has been as a participant-observer, which means that my means of collecting data has been a result of being present at, involved in and recording the routine weekly activities with people in the church or church related settings.[4]

Moreover, my approach to writing the ethnography has used primarily an integrative strategy in which I have attempted to weave together excerpt and interpretation.[5] I have wanted to create a flowing narrative rather than create blocks of examples or interview commentary separate from my own interpretations and analysis. This strategy allows me to present material in a thematic way in order to better illustrate the particular patterns or recurrent themes that emerged over time.

In chapter 5, I delve deeper into the East Bay Church of Religious Science in its particularity. Here, I seek to bring the personality of the church to the foreground by discussing the church within the context of the local communities of which it is a part. I describe the organizational affiliations and structures. I also focus on the minister, presenting her journey from a poor daughter of the rural south to her current position as leader of a large urban church. And I emphasize the congregants themselves, who they are demographically and what roles they occupy within the church community.

In chapter 6, I review some of the social and cultural implications associated with the growing body of African Americans who claim membership in New Thought religions. Additionally, I introduce some of the contemporary African American New Thought ministers who are contributing to the diverse landscape of African American religious expressions, and I consider some remaining questions about the East Bay Church of Religious Science community.

What Is Religious Science?

There is a power for Good in the Universe greater
than you are, and you can use it!

In this book, the East Bay Church of Religious Science
(EBCRS) is the touchstone by which to observe the practical applications of Religious Science. We will see how this
group of African Americans has adapted a religion typically thought of as a religion for Whites to fit their needs
and circumstances. While almost all African Americans
were outside the cultural and social nineteenth-century
New England milieu from which New Thought developed,
the people of EBCRS represent a substantial number of
African Americans who now claim New Thought or Religious Science specifically as their religion.

The minister of the church, the Reverend Elouise Oliver,
("Rev. E"), has stated that the mission of EBCRS is to help
every individual attain a life of wholeness and happiness
that permeates all aspects of life, including health, relationships, and finances. She describes her work as "the business
of raising consciousness through the principles of Religious Science." These teachings and practices affirm that a
person's consciousness is the gateway through which all
things come into being. Whatever a person is experiencing
in the moment is reflective of his or her level of conscious-

ness. Prosperity and well-being manifest themselves in the lives of only those who believe they are possible for them. Those who do not believe in these possibilities must turn to consciousness raising. All persons must get past the mental and emotional issues that are blocking them from experiencing positive results in their lives.

Philosophies such as this are often simplistically relegated to notions about the power of positive thinking. However, Religious Science is supported by cosmological and theological propositions that move it beyond a secular positive thinking system. Likewise, it is distinguished from the sound-alike religions of Scientology and Christian Science. The first response from those unfamiliar with Religious Science is often to associate it with one of these movements. Yet, it is neither the same as Scientology, the movement started by L. Ron Hubbard and popularized by his book *Dianetics* and the many celebrities who ascribe to it; nor is it the same as Christian Science, though the two share some common history and can be considered distant cousins. More of their relationship will be discussed later.

Religious Science shares a historical legacy with many liberal religious traditions such as Unitarian-Universalism, Transcendentalism, and Christian Science, but it is distinct from them as well. Similarly, though Religious Science shares many of the symbols and scriptures of Christianity, it is not a Christian religion in orthodox terms. The founder, Ernest Holmes, sought to remain outside the confines of any one religion but felt free to integrate into his own system the truths he found across the spectrum of religion and philosophy. Consequently, Religious Science can appear to be Christian if individuals choose to practice it as such. As we will see, the East Bay Church of Religious Science borrows heavily from Christianity while also adding its own brand of metaphysical interpretation.

From his youth in rural Maine, Ernest Holmes (1887–1960) was an avid reader and learned to absorb and articulate vast amounts of information. Despite his intellectual curiosity, he left school at fifteen to work and follow his own interests. In 1927 he founded Religious Science, or Science of Mind as it is also called, as a religious and philosophical teaching. He described it as follows:

> Science of Mind represents the correlation of religion, science, and philosophy. We are a religion, in the sense that we explore and teach Universal Principles defining the Spiritual nature of the Universe and our relatedness to God. We are a science, in that students are asked to experiment with these Universal Principles and accept only those which they can prove, demonstrate, or experience in their daily lives. We are a philosophy, in that ideas and ideals are brought together into a system of concepts about God, the Cosmos, humanity, and human possibility.[1]

Furthermore, Religious Science is a denomination of the New Thought religions. The philosophical basis of these various teachings is a metaphysical idealism that affirms the nature of reality to be based upon thoughts or ideas. These teachings hold that in back of all visible forms is the invisible first cause creating through the medium of thought. Moreover, New Thought affirms a pantheistic universe in which all of creation is God in manifestation, and a monistic or unified deity who operates impersonally through principle. Principle is to be understood in this context as "a basic truth or law which has been proved infallible—it works without known exceptions—and impersonal—it works for everyone alike. Science of Mind deals with Spiritual Principles which work the same way—infallibly and impersonally."[2] Followers of these religions believe that one's mental consciousness controls one's life experiences. They teach that it is within each individual's power to raise his or her own consciousness through prayer and affirmative thinking as the means toward attaining fulfillment.

The origin of these teachings in the United States can be traced back to the popular nineteenth-century mental-healing or mind-science phenomenon. Many people in the northeastern United States had already become familiar with and openly curious about Spiritualism, Mesmerism (later to be known as Hypnotism), and Spiritual Healing. These practices, along with the more general religious liberalism of New England, ultimately paved the way for the New Thought religious movement.

By the time Ernest Holmes had come onto the American religious scene, the country had moved through the harsh Puritanism of its founders, undergone the fire and brimstone revivalist teachings of the First Great Awakening, and seen the development of European Enlightenment philosophy, the advance of Transcendentalism and Unitarianism, the evangelistic wave of the Second Great Awakening, and the conversion of African Americans to Christianity in large numbers. Of these movements, New Thought is clearly most closely related to Transcendentalism, with its regard for the individual and the individual's ability to commune with the divine through the recognition of divine omnipresence. Ernest Holmes remained consistent with these roots in his development of Religious Science. Of the transcendentalists, he was most influenced by the writings of Ralph Waldo Emerson. "Having read Emerson it was easy to realize that Unity is at the base of everything."[3] Holmes presented an empowering metaphysical philosophy epitomized by the motto, "There is a power for Good in the Universe greater than you are, and you can use it!"[4] He maintained and built upon the New Thought legacy that it was one's thinking that created one's experiences. He held that the universe was impersonal, scientific, and based upon principles and laws such as cause and effect and the law of attraction. Any idea held in the mind would manifest into experience, whether sickness or health, poverty or prosperity, unhappiness or joy. The impersonal nature of the creative medium would deliver up just what was put into it. Holmes rooted these teachings in the New Testament scripture, "It is done unto you as you believe."[5]

Ernest Holmes owed much to the early leaders of the movement, from whom he learned and borrowed while shaping his own understanding, which he termed Religious Science. Standing at the beginning of the New Thought movement in America was an unassuming healer and teacher named Phineas Parkhurst (P. P.) Quimby. He is generally credited as the founder of New Thought in the United States, thanks to his pioneering work on the theory of mental healing.[6]

In 1802 when Quimby was born in Lebanon, New Hampshire, the religious fervor of the Second Great Awakening was in full swing throughout the Mid-Atlantic States and the South. This period marked a time when African Americans were being converted to evangelical Christianity in large numbers. The intellectual and religious ideas of New England were unknown to rural Blacks, but the underlying basis of those ideas, namely that the universe is sacred and responsive, were indeed part of their worldview as African descendants.

In contrast, Quimby's New England context exposed him to the transcendentalist and spiritualist movements that had become popular in his lifetime. Although he never aligned himself with either of these movements, he lived within a milieu of ideas on individualism, the intuitive nature of the soul, divine revelation outside of orthodox religious structures, mysticism, and clairvoyance. He divided most of his life between stays in the Maine towns of Belfast and Portland. Having had a simple education, he was a clockmaker by trade but was also known to possess great curiosity, savoring the intellectually stimulating environment that nineteenth-century New England provided.

Quimby's own interests centered on mental healing. They were further piqued after he was himself miraculously cured of tuberculosis, a disease that had already taken the lives of many of his family members. His healing inspired him to go on a quest to understand the relationship between illness and health. Quimby began to study and practice Mesmerism and through his own experimentation on volunteers he came to the basis of his theory of mental healing, stating, "I say there is no principle in disease. It is an error that truth can correct."[7] While his method of healing could be perceived as strictly secular, Quimby defined his method as one embodied by Jesus. Making a distinction between Jesus and the Christ, he believed the Christ to be the Wisdom or Truth of God about which Jesus taught and which he used himself.[8] In fact, Quimby felt that he had rediscovered the healing technique of Jesus, having tapped into the same source that Jesus had, thereby manifesting the same effect.

While his theories are the foundation upon which the whole New Thought movement in America rests, he was not a systematic theologian or an organizer of a new religion. His followers came to the forefront as systematizers and organizers. Many in this first group went on to become prominent leaders in New Thought, including Julius Dresser and his wife Annetta Seabury Dresser, Warren Felt

Evans, and Mary Baker Patterson (later Eddy). Each of these students had initially come to Quimby for personal healing and consequently became interested in learning his techniques.[9]

The best known of Quimby's immediate followers was Mary Baker Eddy, who went on to found the First Church of Christ, Scientist (Christian Science). Eddy was the first to organize what may be called a healing ministry around New Thought ideas. Since Quimby left no organization or immediate successor, Eddy's Christian Science organization became the foundation for metaphysical ministries. There is, however, a controversy surrounding Mary Baker Eddy's relationship to P. P. Quimby and about whose work influenced whom. Although she was healed by him and referred favorably to his work as an authentic use of the Christ teaching, she later claimed, after Quimby's death, that her teachings were her own revelation.[10] She further claimed that in fact her revelation was final and that Quimby had learned from her. Her book *Science and Health* was published in 1875 as a philosophy on healing without medicine that she claimed to have discovered herself. The Christian Science organization was formally founded in 1881 in Boston and began to grow from there.

However, a divergence of practice began between Eddy and the Dressers. Julius and Annetta Dresser were also teaching and healing in Boston in 1883. They were following Quimby's still unpublished manuscripts in their practice, utilizing the techniques learned directly from him. As Eddy began to develop and practice more and more of her own theories, the Dressers came to believe that her teachings were inferior to Quimby's. Because all had been Quimby's students, the Dressers knew the source from which Mary Baker Eddy had drawn. They defended the originality of Quimby's thoughts, and the rift between them grew with rather permanent consequences. Eddy began to downplay her association with Quimby and criticized him as having been a mere mesmerist while she had been given the true revelation on Christian healing. This division is still current, with Christian Science and New Thought still being considered separate teachings with separate founders. The fact that New Thought can trace its origins to P. P. Quimby can be attributed to the loyalty and consistency of the Dressers in both their practice and acknowledgments to him. Nevertheless, Mary Baker Eddy's organization of the Christian Science church became a model for other metaphysical teachers as they began institutionalizing their own groups. She established a system of formal training for her ministers that many followers began to use.

Eddy was known to be a strict authoritarian over the dissemination of what she perceived to be her own teachings. The more she heard of others putting their own spin on her techniques, the tighter she held the reins. Consequently, she suffered the disappointment and the loss of many bright Christian Science students who defected from her organization. Some of those who left became well known in their own movements. One of these was Emma Curtis Hopkins. Known to be an independent thinker and mystic, she simply outgrew Eddy's parochial teachings and, after many conflicts between them, they parted company. Hopkins's far-reaching influence on others led her to become known as the teacher's teacher of New Thought leadership.[11] The list of students to whom she ministered included what was to become the leadership of the fully formed New Thought movement, including Malinda E. Cramer, cofounder of Divine Science; Charles and Myrtle Fillmore, founders of the Unity School of Christianity; H. Emilie Cady, author of the Unity textbook, *Lessons in*

Truth; Ella Wheeler Wilcox, poet; and, later, Ernest Holmes, founder of Religious Science.

Hopkins's influence on the formation of the new religious movement has been considerable, though only in recent decades has her formative role been reexamined and highlighted.[12] She is credited by some, such as Gail Harley and Ferne Anderson, as being the true founder of New Thought because of her institutional and educational legacy.[13] Harley emphasizes Hopkins's position as leader, educator, and spiritual mentor to many who went on to found New Thought denominations. While Harley acknowledges that Quimby was a pioneer in the field of mental healing, she questions his status as founder of the religion by noting that he left no institutional following. Harley also maintains that one of the reasons that Hopkins went unnoticed for so long was due to the raging Quimby-Eddy controversy. She was simply eclipsed by Eddy's bolder personality and the sensational news that accompanied it.[14]

One may say that by the early twentieth century the beginning stage of New Thought philosophy had come to a close. The movement was continuing to grow, but with some of its own distinctions. What had been termed mental science or the mental cure was growing into New Thought. Leaders began to reemphasize Quimby's description of his work as having used the same healing methods as Jesus, leading them to requalify the healing techniques as spiritual healing based upon the application of the Christ principle, not simply a mental science. Soon the term "metaphysics" began to be used among leaders in New York and Boston. The word was eventually adopted by the Metaphysical Club in Boston in 1895.[15]

Shifts in vocabulary represented shifts in the movement as well. While the central focus of the movement continued to be on healing, New Thought began to develop as a comprehensive cosmological, philosophical, and theological system beginning around the last decade of the nineteenth century and continuing into the twentieth. The opening of study groups and organizations across the country by various leaders allowed for a certain divergence of interpretation, but there remained consistent threads that held groups and individuals together as members of the New Thought movement. Preeminent among these connective threads are the firmly held beliefs in the unity of God and the unity of all life as individualized expressions of God. These beliefs are echoed throughout the teachings of the movement, whether from the writings of independent thinkers or from established churches. Three denominations arose during this time that still continue to have a strong presence today based upon these fundamental beliefs. Divine Science, Unity, and Religious Science represent the most formalized New Thought denominations in the United States.[16] Many churches prefer to maintain their independence from any institutionalized body, and thus remain outside of these denominations, although they may claim membership in the International New Thought Alliance (INTA) as independent entities.

Ernest Holmes's initial introduction into New Thought was unique from that of most of his predecessors. Since Quimby, people had tended to become attracted to such teachings out of their own need for personal healing. In contrast, Holmes entered this arena because of his own curiosity and initiative. His thought came together through his own independent investigations into metaphysics, psychology, and philosophy. At the time Holmes started serious study of his own, he did not know about the development of the movement, including the writings of Quimby and the Dressers. His knowledge was eclectically gathered and creatively shaped into his own system of "religion, science, and philosophy." He was influenced by Ralph Waldo Emerson, Judge Thomas Troward, Mary Baker Eddy and the Christian Science movement, and by Emma Curtis Hopkins, with whom he studied in 1924 toward the end of her ministry.

Holmes was born in 1887 in Lincoln, Maine, as the youngest of nine boys. Although he lived a rural life with many demanding chores, he became an avid reader early in his youth. His personal habit, from a very young age, was to retire with a book and study it late into the night. The Holmes family kept their own religious rituals with nightly prayers and attendance at a Congregationalist church. Ernest and his brothers were well versed in Bible stories but also enjoyed a religious setting at home free of fire-and-brimstone teaching. Their parents had made a point to counteract any Sunday sermons that preached an eternal damnation for a wretched humanity. Therefore, Ernest grew up in a home where he was free to ask religious questions and where his general inquisitiveness was encouraged.

Holmes's inner drive propelled him to learn all he could, and at the age of twenty he was introduced to Emerson's *Essays,* which remained an important resource to him throughout his life. It was in *Self-Reliance* that young Holmes found validated the idea that a person's own intuition and reason could be of equal value with any other. He learned of the value of independent psychology or what he would later term direct revelation with the divine. From Emerson's *Spiritual Laws,* Holmes began to work out the idea that it was the power of thought that created action. While it is true that Emerson significantly influenced Holmes's thought, it is also true that he did not derive a system of applied metaphysics from reading his books. He learned seminal bits from Emerson that spurred him on to bigger questions and larger understandings of the respective natures of God and humans. His exposure to Emerson prepared him to make use of other writings that were important to his development.

One of these important sources was Mary Baker Eddy and her Christian Science organization, with which he came into contact while living in Boston, where he had begun to take drama classes and perform dramatic recitals. He found most useful in Eddy's work her writings on prayer, which stated that the mental attitude of the person in prayer should be one of faith and thanksgiving, not of petition. He eventually found that the Christian Science movement embodied concepts of dualism, in that Eddy reinforced ideas of good and evil. She taught her followers to guard themselves against the negative thoughts of their enemies because these thoughts had power and could in fact do harm. While Holmes rejected both the idea of separation that would create the concept of an enemy and the idea that one person's thoughts had power over another's, he nevertheless respected the perspectives on prayer that he learned from Christian Science. He began to speak of prayer for the sick as "giving treatments" based upon what he had learned from Eddy's teachings. It was also at this time that he began to expand these ideas around healing into the notion of a spiritual law or principle that could be directly called upon for healing, regardless of religious faith, and that anyone could use. He later wrote:

> This was really a breakthrough in my life. I escaped the bonds of traditional church religion and entered into a new field of consciousness. It was, to be sure, a half-metaphysical use of faith and prayer, but how glorious was that first moment when I consciously used it![17]

Although Holmes continued his work of giving dramatic recitals, he also pursued his interests in the area of New Thought philosophy. Between the years of 1909 and 1919 he began to immerse himself in the writings of Christian D. Larson, Ralph Waldo Trine, and Horatio W. Dresser. Larson's book, *The Ideal Made Real,* was of particular importance for Holmes in that it expanded his thinking about the applicability of the principle into the realm of the "control of conditions through the power of the mind." He had learned from Emerson that his own mind was sufficient to tap into the divine mind that was everywhere present, and Larson's teachings presented him with the idea that this connection could result in "the power to control health, happiness and environment."[18] Larson taught that in order to create one's ideal surroundings, one must mentally picture the Ideal, which would naturally manifest as a result of the law of attraction.

It would still be several years before Ernest Holmes developed his systematic techniques, but he was gathering information from everyone in whom he found truth. By 1910 he was no longer directly using the Christian Science textbook. In its place he had picked up Larson, Trine, and Troward. Judge Thomas Troward, who had been well known as a divisional judge of the Punjab region of Northern India during the era of British colonialism, was one of Holmes's most significant influences. It was Troward who had proclaimed the idea of an infinite, all-encompassing, and neutral principle in the universe. Troward's *Edinburgh Lectures* emphasized the principle of the Universal Unity, which he had learned from his own Vedic studies during his time in India. He further asserted that this Oneness necessarily permeated everything, *and* that this Oneness could be called upon as the Power behind all creative endeavors by anyone to create health and well-being. This

Power was the power in back of all things that healed. It was a Spirit that was available to any who recognized it. Ernest Holmes called it the Universal Mind. He taught that prayer was first a process of attaining harmony with this Oneness, and that all things could be accomplished using this Mind. The neutral principle by which the Mind functioned was the Law. Holmes applied this to his own developing thought and came to understand this idea as the solution to the problem of dualism. The Law simply responds to thoughts held in the Universal Mind, whether they are in harmony with the Universal Mind or not. The Law does not determine whether they are good or bad thoughts, it simply replicates what is held in mind. It is neither judgmental nor punitive. Thus, Holmes taught that dualism is eliminated by understanding the impartiality of the Law. In one of his lectures, he explained, "The way we do it is to impress our thought upon It, and It in turn reacts to us. This is the process by which our thought can be turned to form."[19]

Holmes's application of these teachings was pivotal for both his personal development and his desire to synthesize what he considered to be the highest and best teachings from the philosophies and religions of the world. In 1915 he began to link together his knowledge of Emerson, Troward, Christian Science, New Thought, and Eastern teachings. He believed that significant changes were also happening in Christian theology that reflected new understandings of the human being. He was convinced that the time had come for a new system that joined the best of what had already been presented to humanity. He did not perceive himself to be creating a new religion as such, but as reviving the wisdom that had already come before him and systematizing it in such a way as to make it a practical and scientific teaching that people could use in their own lives.

With this goal in mind, Holmes began lecturing in Los Angeles in 1918 and published his first book, *Creative Mind,* in 1919. His brother Fenwicke shared his interests, and together they began to lecture throughout the country in 1920. Eventually, Ernest decided to remain in the West, where he had gained a large following and established study groups. In 1924 he met Emma Curtis Hopkins, and a new element was added to his developing system. Hopkins, who was now eighty years old, had long been renowned as the definitive teacher on New Thought philosophy. Her particular contribution had been the mystical perspectives that she imparted in her teachings.

Through Hopkins's influence, Holmes's knowledge was expanded beyond the philosophical and theological to include the mystical. She encouraged him to remain focused on the Divine Principle behind all things. The techniques of mental/spiritual healing were not to be confused with the Principle itself. She reminded Holmes to keep his attention on the First Cause: to worship in Spirit and in Truth. He applied her advice to the formulation of his scientific method of prayer, calling it a treatment. Treatments were based upon the Practitioner's purposeful connection to the Universal Spirit in such a way as to declare the health and well-being of any person from the perspective of the Ideal or perfect Universal Pattern that exists for every created thing. In a somewhat mystical way, the Practitioner could unify with the divine and declare perfect health and well-being from the perspective of the Divine Perfection. Religious Science Practitioners would refer to this as speaking the word of Truth about a situation. The Truth, in this sense, is that God is whole, perfect, and complete, and therefore everyone and everything else in its essence is whole, perfect, and complete as well. The acknowledgment of this Truth could be used to correct any situation whatsoever. Ernest Holmes met with Emma Curtis Hopkins only a few times, but her influence helped him to develop the technique of Spiritual Mind Treatments as one of the cornerstones of Science of Mind practice.

In 1926 Holmes published the *Science of Mind* textbook, which defined and articulated the principles of Religious Science. It is still in use as the definitive sourcebook for Religious Science churches today, along with the monthly publication, *Science of Mind.* In 1927 Holmes founded the Institute of Religious Science for the purpose of training Practitioners who could help him meet the demand of those in need of spiritual mind treatment. While Holmes never intended to start a church (he believed this would lead to a dogmatic religion), others around him petitioned for such status as small groups began to form and grow. Due to this call, the early 1940s became a time of institutional development with organizational plans, chapter bylaws, qualification policies for Practitioners, and ministerial ordinations being established. The Church of Religious Science was established formally in 1953. Today, Religious Science has splintered into two main groups, United Church of Religious Science and Religious Science International, and two newer, smaller bodies, Affiliated New Thought Churches of Religious Science and Global Religious Science Ministries.

Religious Science is probably the most systematic of all New Thought denominations. I became profoundly aware of this when I began a fifteen-week course of study at the East Bay Church of Religious Science called the "Foundations" class. This course, which Reverend E always coteaches, is open to all in the church community and covers the history and principles of Religious Science. The class met from 7:00 p.m. to 10:00 p.m. on Tuesday nights from October 2000 to January 2001. We began with eighty-six

people, but lost ten or so along the way. Those who drop
the class and want to retake it are required to wait for a new
class and start over, no matter how far they made it
through the previous class. Each class began with a meditation, followed by team teaching from Reverend E and a
Practitioner, group discussion and exercises, and small
"pod" group discussions of about ten people in which individual concerns and homework were discussed. The classes
ended with a benediction. The weekly course work included reading from the student manual, completing written exercises, and calling our respective pod group leaders
with a spiritual mind treatment. As the course progressed
we took quizzes, a final exam, and conducted individual
presentations that represented the most significant core
concept we had learned to integrate into our lives.[20]

By taking the class I learned the principles of Religious
Science at a much deeper level than I had learned while attending services. The teachings are extensive; yet their systematic presentation has simplified the explanation of its
doctrine into two generalized categories: the "thing itself"
and the way it works. The "thing itself" is a term that refers
to the basic cosmological and theological beliefs of Religious Science adherents. It is a tool that attempts to provide an objective description of the nature of God and the
cosmos. It reveals the working-out of the theological questions, what is God and how does the universe work? The
way it works refers to the practical application of the principle to human life. It is the tool that provides the knowledge one needs to make individual use of the principle, attempting to answer the questions, How does the abstract
show up in human life and how can people use these principles to improve their situations?

The first essential principle of Religious Science describes the thing itself as God, variously referred to as the

Universal Mind, one Supreme Being, one Fundamental Reality Principle, one Infinite Source of all that is. All creation is made up of One substance, God is this Oneness, and thus God is all there is. The way it works follows this unity principle and extends it to describe the nature of human beings. Each human being is one with God, an individualized expression of the one God. Human beings represent an incarnation of the Spirit in flesh. This was not an experience limited to Jesus but is the reality of all people. Spirit is the essence of creation and it is inherently good.

The thing itself is further described as having a macrocosmic threefold nature: Spirit, Soul, and Body. Spirit is Conscious Mind, the Love-Intelligence that selects or initiates action. Soul is the Creative Medium, the receptive but neutral Law, moving only in direct response to the dictates of Spirit. Thus, it is explained that Love and Law govern the universe. Body is simply the manifestation of thought; it is mind in form. Consequently, it is said that the manifest universe is the body of God.

This concept is essential for understanding the divine creative continuum in which human beings share. The continuum describes the unceasing creative process that starts in the Universal Mind, which is God, as a thought; this thought is then impressed upon the Law or Creative Medium, which operates as impersonally as soil receiving a seed; this thought then manifests itself as material form, just as a seed sprouts into a plant of its own kind. This is the method by which God created and continues to create the manifest universe; thus, it is the method by which human beings create their own individual realities as well. Holmes wrote, "The Universe is the result of the self-contemplation of God. Our lives are the result of our self-contemplations, and are peopled with the personifications of our thoughts and ideas."[21] Rev. E described it this way:

We all use the same stuff to co-create, there is only one type of God-stuff and each individual uses it to their specificity. Same stuff, different forms. We share the mind of God. We do not have individual minds, but individual uses of God's mind and we re-enact the same creative process that God uses.[22]

In terms of the Universal Principle, human beings possess this same threefold nature in microcosm. People initiate the same creative process at the level of Spirit by focusing on a thought or selecting an action to take. At the Soul level or in the Creative Medium, the thought is unconsciously subjected to the beliefs we already hold personally or the beliefs we share with the race, resulting in the manifestation of our thoughts as we really believe them through the working of the Law. For example, if a particular woman wants a new job but feels lacking in her professional abilities and believes no one will hire her, or she believes that the job market is scarce, then her experience will be that she will not find a new job. In short, this teaching presupposes an intelligent and responsive universe. Science of Mind espouses that thoughts held consciously (in spirit) gestate in the soil of the thoughts already held to be true (soul) and will therefore become embodied in corresponding positive or negative form.

Religious Science seeks to teach a reliable system for creating positive life experiences. Its approach is to raise the consciousness of its adherents to a level of personal empowerment and responsibility grounded in the idea that human beings are created in the image and likeness of God even to the extent that individuals have the same creative power in the microcosm that God has in the macrocosm. It is taught that once this unity is recognized, the Universal Mind can be utilized by anyone to create a life abundant in health, wealth, and happiness. In fact, Religious Science teaches that human beings are always creating their own experiences whether they are conscious of it or not. It is the conscious use of the Universal Mind that allows people to consistently (i.e., scientifically) create desired experiences. If individuals are only unconsciously using this Universal Mind, then at best they live in a world of seeming random events, coincidences, and luck or, at worst, a world of unhappiness, disease, lack, and limitation. Holmes taught these ideas as an interpretation of Jesus' teachings. He wrote, "We are surrounded by a Creative Mind which reacts to our thought. This is the basis of all faith and all effective prayer." This is why Jesus told us that when we pray we should believe we already have what we desire. When Jesus said that it is done unto us as we believe, he implied that there is a Power that can, will, and must react to us.[23]

In order to make use of the Universal Mind, both consciously and scientifically, Religious Science teaches a three-step approach: affirmation, spiritual mind treatment, and meditation, (a-t-m). These methods are the tools by which individuals change their thinking. They are ways of rooting out old, dysfunctional thought patterns and replacing them with new, more positive ones. For example, an "affirmation is a desire stated in present tense terms as if it is already manifest in one's life."[24] Participants are asked to claim their desires or state their claims of well-being even in the face of contrary feelings. Such feelings should be examined and recognized as not being consistent with one's desires and thus reprogrammed via affirmations. These are the beliefs that have previously manifested themselves in one's life but have remained hidden from conscious thought, thereby causing seemingly random or negative experiences. The use of affirmations helps believers to recognize these hidden beliefs and to create more desirable experiences.

Spiritual Mind Treatment, acknowledged by followers as the most powerful technique that Science of Mind teaches, is also known as affirmative prayer. This method of prayer is not carried out in a petitioner mode or from a mental position of lack, asking God to bestow something upon the person praying or to perform a miracle on his or her behalf. This would portray God as arbitrary, granting mercy and special favor to a select few. To the contrary, Religious Science teaches that God operates impartially through the impersonal nature of the Law, therefore one must approach prayer from this different perspective. "Affirmative prayer is not supplication or petition, but recognition and acceptance that God is all there is; and that all the abundance of the universe is already ours if we accept and embody it."[25] Treatments consist of five steps: recognition, unification, declaration, thanksgiving, and release. The first two steps are regarded by many Religious Scientists as the two most important ones as they are akin to meditation, whereby one acknowledges the Oneness of God and one's own unity with God.

> Their function is to assist you in bringing your consciousness to the highest level possible at any given time. In your knowing of the Allness of God and your Oneness with it, you are able to turn completely from the condition about which you are treating and realize the Spiritual Truth of it.[26]

Thus, these two steps are considered sufficient to manifest whatever may be desired because all illusions of separation have been overcome.

The third step is the declarative stage of stating the object or condition of one's desire. This statement is really an affirmation. It is the point of claiming and accepting the desired outcome with faith and conviction that it is already accomplished. In the last two stages, the practitioner gives thanks in the knowledge that the prayer is complete and then releases the prayer without any further worry or concern over the situation. It is then given over to God in the form of Universal Law, with the expectation that the prayer will manifest itself accordingly.

Spiritual Mind Treatment can be done for oneself, for another whether present or not, or by a Practitioner of the church. It is taught as a powerful tool for consciously creating one's own reality, moving people away from the idea that they are victims of circumstance or powerless to achieve their goals. It reflects Ernest Holmes's systemization of earlier Spiritual Mind healers all the way back to P. P. Quimby. Holmes studied their methods and their results and concluded that anyone could put these techniques into practice for themselves. His Science of Mind represents his attempt at putting this process in the hands of the average person in a practical and reliable fashion. As he explained it,

Unless there were a definite method of procedure in spiritual mind healing, it could not be considered scientific. Unless a definite technique could be delivered, there would be no intelligent approach to the subject. Unless one could learn the technique and consciously apply it, it would not be universally applicable. But the Science of Mind is just as definitely scientific and just as positively based on an actual principle as any other science.[27]

Moreover, treatment is not to be understood as a way of manipulating people or coercing God. Rather, it is a technique for "allowing God's power to flow through [the individual] into manifestation of the Truth, without hindrance from false beliefs."[28] It is also not a method of denying physical illness or suffering. Followers of Religious Science are encouraged to use all methods of healing that are available to them. Treatment is one way toward health because it allows for "the conscious clearing away of the grime of false beliefs from a condition to reveal the Truth that was always there."[29] Such false beliefs would be any that reflect lack, limitation, or separation from the Unity of God, which manifest as illness, poverty and suffering. Treatment serves to remind the individual of the "Truth" of his/her oneness with God, thus dispelling the "grime" of unwanted thoughts and conditions.

Finally, meditation is taught and encouraged as a means of listening to God. Affirmation and treatment are initiated by the individual as a means of either talking to oneself or to God; but meditation is the act of being still and quiet, to be able to listen to the guidance that comes from within. It is a tool by which practitioners may acknowledge the unity principle, which then informs all other thoughts and activities.

Many students have raised the obvious question, "What about when the desired manifestation still does not show up?" The answer from the church is to continue to apply the principles, "do not be deterred." Rev. E admonishes, "Monitor your own thoughts and root out the negative ones. Replace them with affirmations and express gratitude as if your goal is already accomplished. Notice that any shift in circumstances means your prayers are being answered."

The other common question relates to the human predicament. How does the Science of Mind respond to questions of death, pain, and suffering? What about when bad things happen to good people? Does evil exist? The answers hearken back to the principle of unity espoused throughout Religious Science teaching. There is no duality in this system, and evil exists only as a misuse of the creative process, it has no substance or power of its own. Reminiscent of the Christian *privatio boni* doctrine that pronounced evil as having no being of its own, Science of Mind teaches that evil does not exist as such.[30] Furthermore, this philosophy has no developed doctrine on an endtime or an afterlife. A doctrine of immortality is affirmed, because God "knows only Life, its eternal continuity, evolution, and expansion," but there is no teaching about the experiences of an afterlife. It is assumed that spirit always continues in some form, but Religious Science offers no details on what form the afterlife may take. Death is viewed as a passing over into a different dimension of spiritual being in which human flesh is not necessary. Just as a baby is conceived and born into the human dimension with flesh, living things also pass back into the spiritual realm of the God essence from which all life comes forth without material form.

Science of Mind assumes the existential situation of humankind to be that of spiritual beings having human experiences. It proclaims that humans are of a spiritual essence and represent incarnations of that spirit in human flesh. Humans are of the same substance as God, because God is all there is, thus followers are encouraged to recognize the indwelling God in others and in themselves. This means that people are viewed as children of God, all of whom are heirs to the abundance of the kingdom. Anything that compromises the manifestation of prosperity and well-being results in pain and suffering, but these are not the conditions inherent to humanity. Therefore, the human predicament as people generally experience it with pain and suffering is not the result of an original sin, rather it is the result of ignorance. The teachings of Religious Science encourage individuals to acknowledge their own true spiritual identity, and in so doing to accept their position as rightful inheritors of all that God has to offer. This thought is expressed as follows:

> We live in an abundant Universe; everything in nature is giving of itself. Jesus taught that God's good pleasure is to give us the kingdom, but we can partake of this great generosity only to the extent that we are able to receive. We need not remain ignorant of God's willingness to provide for us.[31]

And further, taken from an Ernest Holmes meditation:

> Since I know the Truth of my being, I will no longer hinder or retard my good from coming to me. I will expect and accept all that I need to make life happy and worthwhile; for I am a child of the Spirit, and every attribute of it—every attribute of Good is my inheritance.[32]

Holmes further taught that evil in itself is nonexistent. It has no substance, since it is understood that God is all there is, encompassing all paradoxes, all seeming contradictions. There is no power in the universe other than God. It is acknowledged that people experience pain and suffering, but this is a diminished mental state and/or a misuse of the universal principles, which often result in manifestations rooted in feelings of self-condemnation. Religious Science principles are offered to correct these misuses. Holmes offered the following statement:

> In the Science of Mind we do not say everything is alright when it is all wrong. We do not say peace when there is no peace, but rather we try to discover what is wrong and why

we do not have peace. We do not say that people are not poor, sick or unhappy. We ask why these things should be if the Original cause of all things is Harmonious, Perfect, Radiant and happy.[33]

Moreover, Religious Science does not affirm a doctrine of original sin; rather, it is taught that God sees the good in God's own creation. God is not keeping track of individual misdeeds but allows everyone to make his or her own free choices. "We are not punished for our mistakes, but by them, through the impersonal action of the Law—there is no forgiveness or unforgiveness in God, only justice without judgment according to the impersonal consequences of our choices."[34] The law of cause and effect reflects the individual's own beliefs. Rev. E affirms this in her teaching as well. She often states, "God does not inflict punishment. Suffering arises from the false belief of separation from God which then results in feelings of lack, fear, loneliness and anger."[35]

Consequently, conflict arises in the mind when one imagines that some actions are "sinful" or result in a separation from God. Science of Mind teaches that there is nothing separate from God; God encompasses all seeming opposites, so that even those things that appear "evil" remain within the context of God. God is an infinite paradox of love and law in action. Love allows the freedom of choice, and law responds accordingly. If a person feels victimized by fate, or unfairly burdened with hardships, Science of Mind responds with the following:

When we stop making the mistake, we are automatically forgiven; but, of course, we will be punished by a mistake while we continue in it. However, let no intelligent person say that, because the spirit knows no sin, there is no

mistake made by the human or the individual mind. . . .
And when we have transcended previous mistakes they no
longer exist, nor is there any effect of them. This means a
complete salvation from the *sin* which was the *mistake*, and
the *punishment* which was the *consequence*.[36] (Author's ital-
ics)

Thus, the Science of Mind suggests to its followers that the
appropriate response to the appearance of evil in their lives
is based upon the idea of *metanoia*, or repentance by means
of changing one's mind. The phrase that Jesus used in his
healings "to go and sin no more" is understood to embody
this principle. For he understood that when a person
changed his or her actions and beliefs, a change in experiences would necessarily follow, in accordance with the universal principle of cause and effect and the law of attraction.

Religious Science now stands as one of the contemporary bastions of New Thought philosophy. Its founder took
the philosophical and religious teachings of many who had
come before him, and coalesced them into a systematic formula for well-being. It was important to Ernest Holmes
that his teaching not be exclusive, and that anyone could
apply the principles within the context of their own religious beliefs and still make good use of Religious Science.
The following "Declaration of Principles" represents the
closest thing to a definitive creed to be found on the belief
system of Religious Science. The East Bay Church of Religious Science uses it as the responsive reading at each service.

We believe in God, the Living Spirit Almighty: one inde-
structible absolute and self-existent Cause. This One manifests Itself in and through all creation, but is not absorbed

by Its Creation. The manifest universe is the body of God; it is the logical and necessary outcome of the infinite self-knowingness of God.

We believe in the incarnation of the Spirit in all and that we are all Incarnations of the One Spirit.

We believe in the eternality, the immortality and the continuity of the Individual soul, forever and ever expanding.

We believe that the Kingdom of Heaven is within us and that we experience this Kingdom to the degree that we become conscious of it.

We believe the ultimate goal of all life to be a complete emancipation from all discord of every nature, and that this goal is sure to be attained by all.

We believe in the unity of all life, and that the highest God and the innermost God is one God.

We believe that God is personal to all who feel this Indwelling Presence.

We believe in the direct revelation of Truth through our intuitive and spiritual nature, and that anyone may become a revealer of Truth who lives in close contact with the Indwelling God.

We believe that the Universal Spirit, which is God, operates through a Universal Mind, which is the law of God, and that we are surrounded by this Creative Mind which receives the direct impress of our thought and acts upon it.

We believe in the healing of the sick through the power of this Mind.

We believe in the control of conditions through the power of this Mind.

We believe in the eternal Goodness, the eternal Loving-Kindness and the eternal Givingness of life to all.

We believe in our own soul, our own spirit and our own destiny; for we understand that the life we live is God. And so it is.[37]

These principles are meant to convey to the worshipper a sense of unity with God, and to remind them that unification is the doorway through which change can happen. By beginning the church services with this statement, Rev. E seeks to create a space in which individual transformation may occur for her congregation members. Each of these principles is understood to be important for raising consciousness beyond the visible circumstances of one's life. They are meant to help people stop thinking about the problem and get them to refocus upon God. Religious Science churches teach that it is the false concept of separation from God that is at the root of all disharmonies in a person's life. Followers believe that change begins by acknowledging God first. Consequently, all prayer treatments begin by acknowledging this unity principle. Throughout the book we will be engaged with the East Bay Church of Religious Science and how the congregation embodies religious and philosophic principles such as these.

2

Historical Intersections and New Religious Adaptations

> You need to be in a church that says you are blessed, you are prosperous.[1]

While New Thought had its origins in the New England milieu of Mind Science, Spiritualism, Unitarianism, Transcendentalism, and various other types of liberal religious ideas, African Americans were largely located in the South, living on plantations. Before the Second Great Awakening (1790–1830), the religious practices of most African Americans had been limited to their experiences on the plantation under the category of "slave religion." If the slave owner was permissive, the slaves could be baptized as Christians and have their own meetings. In that context, African Americans were far removed from the New England intellectualism that spawned New Thought. However, they would not remain permanently outside the reach of these teachings. The urban migrations of the 1920s and 1930s would introduce many African Americans to New Thought principles, eventually fostering the development of churches like the East Bay Church of Religious Science.

African Americans' religious history demonstrates that they were a people who could reenvision their religious realities. From their early experiences with Christianity and "hush-harbor" slave religion, they would seek religious expressions that served their goals for freedom and justice.[2] As transplanted Africans who found themselves in harsh circumstances among foreign people and foreign religions, they began to construct, over time, African American religions that would provide tools for self-preservation, protest, and even revolt.

While the African and Euro-American cultures were influencing one another, Black religion remained distinct from its White counterpart through its pervasive emphasis on freedom and justice.[3] The sociologist Joseph Washington affirms that it was through the advent of Black folk religion that African Americans found support and created means by which to change their circumstances. Folk religion, he wrote, is focused upon seeking the freedom and equality of Black people, and the pursuit of this ideal became the reason for the development of independent Black churches. "While the white man was using religion to keep the slaves content, Negroes were using their meetings to sow discontent and provide the means of revolt and escape."[4] Black churches became the initial institutions for championing survival, self-determination, and liberation. These churches took on a central position for African Americans as the stronghold against White domination and racial oppression. Even as slaves, African Americans began to exercise some degree of freedom in the religious realm constructing their own songs, rituals, and worship styles. The independent Black churches that developed provided a multitude of services for African Americans, a distinguishing factor from White churches whose members had the benefit of multiple social resources. The Black churches provided educational and economic support for the Black communities, as well as encouragement for self-help and determination.

Consequently, the institutionalized, independent Black Christian churches have been the dominant voice for African American religious expressions. The traditional conceptualization of the Black church reflects the major denominations—the Baptists, Methodists, and Pentecostals, along with their respective sectarian bodies.[5] Lincoln and Mamiya estimate that more than 80 percent of Black Christians belong to one of these denominations.[6] It is important to note the historical and contemporary diversity of African American religious practices, exemplified by a New Thought church like the East Bay Church of Religious Science. We must not lose sight of the various creative ways in which African Americans of the past and the present have reconstructed their religious systems to remain meaningful within the context of their New World challenges. The shifts in worldview that African people had to make upon their arrival in North America resulted in syncretism on many levels, notably in religion. Their adjustments are representative of what it means to live and survive in the context of American society in which cultures and histories continually intersect and depart in new directions.

During the early to middle decades of the twentieth century, many African Americans left the South for better employment opportunities in the urban North. As the influx of European immigrants began to subside, the growing industrial economy pulled many African Americans up from the economically depressed rural South.[7] However, as these migrants arrived in the big cities, they often found themselves socially overwhelmed and out of place. Life had shifted for most of them from a small-town agrarian lifestyle to that of an anonymous, industrialized metropolis.

Not only was this migration of African Americans socially significant, it also produced some important religious phenomena, such as the rise of the so-called Black Gods of the Metropolis and the profusion of nontraditional "storefront" churches.[8] Because urban churches were often large and impersonal many new city-dwellers felt at loose ends. These migrants met their new challenges by becoming religiously innovative, much as their ancestors had done before them. The nonmainstream religious expressions seemed to fill a gap in the experiences of transplanted African Americans.[9] These expressions have notable affinities with New Thought religious practices.

During the 1920s and 1930s, New Thought leaders, predominantly if not exclusively White, had not involved themselves with the race issues of the times. However, a number of African American religious leaders of the period embraced general New Thought principles and shaped them to fit the needs of their congregations of mostly poor, Black, powerless people. These leaders saw value in preaching self-determination, affirmative prayer, and prosperity much the same as people like Ernest Holmes had seen it. Whereas Holmes sought a universal application for the Religious Science philosophy, African American leaders were applying New Thought principles with laserlike precision to the specific needs of their followers. They directed these universal teachings to address the particular problems Black people were facing. Through the leadership of ministers like Father Hurley, Father Divine, Rev. Ike, and Daddy Grace, African Americans were being helped by New Thought principles despite the silence from New Thought leaders on civil rights issues. While benefiting from these principles, African Americans were more often experiencing these teachings under the rubric of prosperity preaching rather than the term "New Thought." The ministers that Black people knew from their neighborhoods told them the keys to health and wealth were self-value and self-determination. Ensconced within the more familiar Spiritual and/or Pentecostal religious practices, the teachings were readily accepted by many urban African Americans as a prelude to membership in New Thought religions such as Unity and Religious Science.

Urban Developments and New Thought Affinities with African American Spiritualism and Pentecostalism

African Americans began to get a taste of New Thought teachings through various Spiritual and Pentecostal-style urban ministries. While these churches did not call themselves New Thought, the content of their messages was very similar to what had come out of New England. They encouraged their followers to be self-determinant, to think positively, and to perform specific prayers and rituals for the attainment of their desires. They taught their followers that money was good and that they should expect to lead fulfilling and abundant lives here on Earth. Reviewing some of the parallels between New Thought and these Black urban religious traditions, we can see some of the specific adaptations that African American believers have made to their religious lives in light of their particular challenges, and discover what some have found compelling about New Thought religions such as Religious Science today.

Both New Thought and Spiritualism are regarded as thaumaturgical sects—religious practices that encourage followers to take a role in controlling their environments and experiences through the performance of some type of religious ritual or specific type of prayer.[10] Such rituals acknowledge an ultimate reality that exists beyond the five senses and invite the energies of these realms to participate with the believers in changing their circumstances. For example, a believer with a recurrent illness may be told to say a certain prayer under specific conditions and then not to think or worry about it again. "After you have said your prayer, give it over to God." These groups teach followers that they can attain the good life (e.g., health, wealth, and success) by connecting with the divine through prayer or the use of special objects or both. These sects concern themselves with the concrete problems of their adherents or clients by providing them with spiritual means for acquiring needed finances, employment, health, emotional tranquility, love, or the reconciliation of a strained social relationship.[11]

Within the realm of African American religious studies, Black Spiritualism is recognized as the largest group of these sects. Some sociologists have described these churches as being particularly attractive to communities of mostly poor and oppressed people who may already feel disenfranchised from educational and employment opportunities. The rituals of Black Spiritual churches have brought a sense of potency to the poor by promising that benefits may be obtained through the performance of special rituals and positive thinking.[12]

We can understand African American Spiritualism as an eclectic mix of religious traditions. At the core are elements of Catholicism, Vodun, Black Protestantism, and New Thought. African American Spiritualism differs in emphasis from its White counterpart. Blacks initially found American spiritualism of the nineteenth century appealing, but sought to adapt it to fit their own worldview.[13] The practice of communication with the spirit world was a familiar concept to many African Americans who felt some resonance with this aspect of traditional African religious practice. In addition, the relatively open racial policy was an inviting proposition to many Blacks who joined the New England variety of Spiritualism at this time.

As with their adaptive approach to Protestantism, African Americans began to reshape this Spiritualism to better serve their own circumstances. We see examples in the development of the National Colored Spiritualist Association established in Detroit in 1922. The Black Spiritual movement broke away from the White-controlled National Spiritualist Association of Churches at this time.[14] Some early congregations existed in relative isolation, but it was not until the 1920s that Black Spiritual churches began to appear in greater numbers in cities like Chicago, Nashville, Detroit, New Orleans, and New York. This expansion is consistent with the migration patterns of African Americans, which began to increase following the First World War and continued in waves from the 1940s to 1960s.

Many African Americans began to migrate to the North for the promise of better lives. While they achieved this goal in some ways, it was also true that these urban areas were not accommodating to masses of Black people. The barriers of racism were still in place and often resulted in the ghettoization of the African Americans who had come in the hope of improving their circumstances. Racism, unemployment, and underemployment led to cycles of poverty, disenfranchisement, and disillusionment. The types of social crises emerging from the northern migrations caused Black religion to become even more diversified than it had been since the development of independent Black churches. The Black Spiritualists, for example, developed as one of the many ways that churchgoing Blacks responded to the racist and stratified structure of a capitalist society in which they were blocked from fully participating.

Black Spiritualist churches often existed as small "storefront" groups holding services in private homes or in commercial property. People were often attracted to these churches more than the larger, established ones because they had smaller congregations, allowing for more intimate social connections and personal recognition and an evangelical worship style that was reminiscent of their former home churches. These more intimate spaces allowed many Blacks to feel free to express themselves with shouting, holy dancing, and singing spirituals. Often they also found the preaching style more to their liking.

An interesting phenomenon was that many leaders in the Spiritualist churches gave themselves royal titles and officiating positions such as King, Queen, Prince, Princess, or Royal Elect Ruler. The churches provided an atmosphere of status and security that contrasted the menial or subservient roles that many Blacks assumed while living in the shadows of White supremacy.[15] Spiritual churches responded by providing a place for authentic being and control of one's affairs.

Although there are many points of intersection between Black Protestantism and Spiritualism, it is the emphasis on controlling and manipulating one's immediate condition through the use of religious practices that distinguishes Spiritualism from the more conventional religious sects such as Holiness or Pentecostal. Most often these practices include burning of particular candles or incense, praying before an icon of a saint, using consecrated objects, divining by a medium, and laying on of hands for physical healings.

Many who attend spiritual churches are not members or even regular attendees, but they come for the occasional "bless" or demonstration services. These services are intended to offer specific rituals for helping people achieve their goals, for example, for money, employment, relationships, or improved health. In addition, believers often seek the services of the ministers, also known as prophets, mediums, and healers, in individual consultation. Believers and visitors alike often seek out spiritualism because of its positive thinking ideology. Spiritualism addresses many of the most visceral problems and needs of its followers by offering immediate solutions. People can take something home with them from a service or focus upon their prayer work in a certain way and feel that they are creating change in their lives.

We can begin to see some affinities between Spiritualism and New Thought religions in a number of ways. Apart from any emphasis on communication with the dead that is often part of Spiritualism, there are some consistencies between these religious systems. Clearly there are shared emphases on affirmative thinking, spiritual healing, and the use of rituals or special knowledge for bringing about personal success. While the religious systems may differ in methodology, they find common ground in affirming the power of individuals to direct their own circumstances by the power of their thoughts and the performance of specified actions. Some of the historically known Spiritual leaders of the urban North, the so-called Black Gods of the Metropolis, including Father Hurley, Father Divine, Rev. Ike and Daddy Grace, have specifically incorporated New Thought concepts and practices into their ministries. These men were the early representatives of New Thought principles in Black urban America.

A common characteristic of Spiritual congregations in northern American cities is the veneration of the church's founder.[16] This is also the case with the aforementioned individuals. Each of these leaders became known for preaching a message of living an abundant life in the here and now to a largely poor and working-class segment of the African American population. While each was known for his own brand of eccentricity, personal flamboyance or ostentatious services, each one also taught self-empowerment and self-improvement through a combination of positive affirmations and ritualistic use of objects. For example, Father Hurley, founder of the Universal Hagar's Spiritual Churches in 1923, and his better-known contemporary, Father Divine, founder of the Peace Mission, heralded themselves as incarnations of God. Both used their ministries to focus on the needs of poor Blacks. Father Hurley, considered by his followers, the Hurleyites, to be the founder of true Spiritualism, was known to be a dynamic activist in the struggle for African American civil rights as early as the 1920s. Often purveyors of a nationalist political agenda, the religious leadership of his ministry encouraged his followers to practice positive thinking and to work toward changing their own lives. He offered the same faith in the power of positive thinking to poor Blacks that Dale Carnegie and Norman Vincent Peale would later successfully market to Whites in a secular fashion. Moreover, Hurley offered his followers an elaborate system of rituals, incantations, and occult knowledge intended to provide them with spiritual power to overcome their circumstances.[17] His prescriptions differed from New Thought only in degree, not in kind. During Hurley's time, Divine Science and Unity were fully formed New Thought churches teaching their followers to ritualistically perform prayers and affirmations to bring about desired changes in circumstances. Meanwhile, Ernest Holmes was incubating his ideas of spiritual mind treatment for the purpose of helping people to change their lives under the system of Religious Science.

Father Divine's Peace Mission included up to 160 churches during its heyday from the Depression to the early 1940s throughout the United States and internationally. Much like many of the early New Thought leaders, his ministry began with healing.[18] Father Divine began a healing practice in 1931 in Sayville, Long Island, and later moved to Philadelphia in 1942. His ministry encompassed a social reform emphasis that included providing food, clothing, and educational services to the poor. One of his trademarks was his elaborate banquets, which lasted an entire day. These feasts represented the type of abundance and prosperity that he taught his followers to seek, also characteristic of New Thought religions. One of the many biographies on Father Divine reports that "the Peace Mission promoted visualization of the positive as its philosophical basis."[19] His philosophy was recognized as a merging of elements from Catholicism, Pentecostalism, Methodism, and positive thinking. Father Divine's emphasis upon visualization and affirmations of abundance and health helped his followers to understand their own creative power. Though his ministry was primarily (if nontraditionally) Christian, he helped to bring New Thought principles to African Americans who accepted them as a means for improving their circumstances during the turbulent Depression era. Since the death of Father Divine in 1965, the number of Peace Mission churches has continued on a much smaller scale, with five main churches located along the Northeastern seaboard. These churches have branches and subsidiaries throughout the country and abroad.[20]

The Reverend Ike is another of the Black Gods of the Metropolis whose message dovetailed with that of key Black Spiritualists. Although he was not a member of the Spiritual tradition strictly speaking, his prominent stature among thaumaturgical sects cannot be overlooked since he is arguably the best-known leader of any in this group.

Moreover, his ministry clearly represents a historical intersection between New Thought teachings and African American religious expressions. As the self-proclaimed "Success and Prosperity Preacher," Rev. Ike's philosophy is self-image psychology. He teaches that "through positive self awareness the individual can change the conditions and circumstances in his or her own life."[21] Born Frederick J. Eikerenkoetter II in 1935, he was brought up in the Holiness and Pentecostal traditions. When he began to minister at age fourteen, his message was a product of those practices, including biblical literalism, strict morality, and speaking in tongues. However, Rev. Ike felt that he had not distinguished himself enough from other evangelist-style preachers. His approach did not garner him the type of success and recognition that he wanted for himself, and thus he embraced the flamboyant personal style that became his trademark. The period 1969–1972 marked a transition for Rev. Ike, after which time New Thought became an established basis of his message. His teachings began to emphasize positive thinking, an indwelling God, the notion that thoughts govern behavior, an approval of monetary and material acquisitiveness, and a rejection of the traditional Christian doctrine of sin.[22] His formula, visualization, affirmation, and meditation are familiar techniques to all practitioners of New Thought religions. A core practice of Religious Science, for example, is affirmation, treatment, and meditation for the purpose of centering oneself spiritually, allowing the desired circumstances to manifest. Rev. Ike has been in ministry since the 1950s and claims to have reached millions of people.[23] His current platforms are his Christ United Church, based in New York City since 1969, and his syndicated televangelist program broadcast over ten major television stations and more than ninety-two radio stations.

While each of these leaders found a substantial following at one time or another, the larger Black community often considered them frauds who took advantage of the poor and less-educated Blacks of urban ghettoes.[24] Nevertheless, each of these figures encouraged people to grow beyond their immediate circumstances, and to believe in their own worth and abilities. Though their methods may have been unorthodox, each contributed an important piece to the African American religious mosaic, creating a precedent for African American followers of New Thought principles. The empowering notion that a person, even a poor Black person, could control his or her circumstances had been received by the collective psyche. These preachers adapted and redirected nineteenth-century Spiritualism and New Thought teachings for the Black metropolises.

In addition to the Spiritual churches, Pentecostalism was, and continues to be, an influential religious practice among African Americans. Black thaumaturgical sects often draw a significant part of their evangelical style from Pentecostalism. A primary example of this was Daddy Grace. His ministry reflected practices from both Pentecostalism in moral code, ecstatic worship styles, and the thaumaturgical traditions with their emphases on spiritual healing and religious rituals. He is the bridge between the Pentecostal tradition and its affinities with New Thought. Moreover, we will later see that some of these elements are found in the belief system and worship style of the East Bay Church of Religious Science, contributing to its uniqueness among Religious Science churches.

Daddy Grace was born Marcelino Manoel da Graca in 1881 of Afro-Portuguese heritage. Using the name Charles Emmanuel (or Manuel) Grace, he moved to New Bedford, Massachusetts, in 1900, starting his United House of Prayer for All People there in 1921. This church was established among mostly poor African Americans, but it had a small percentage of Whites as well. Daddy Grace soon began to establish churches beyond Massachusetts, and had much success among economically depressed areas of the South, such as North Carolina and Virginia. His movement continued to grow in the North as well, with churches in Brooklyn, Manhattan, and Detroit. Though personally flamboyant in appearance, he taught a strict moral code that prohibited drinking, smoking, tobacco, card playing, gambling, and social dancing. Incorporating elements from the Pentecostals, he encouraged dancing only in the worship of God, along with singing, shouting, ecstatic bodily contortions, and testifying.

Following the Pentecostal tradition, members were expected to have had a conversion experience through the Holy Spirit. Conversion would result in sanctification or living a purified life in which individuals no longer commit sins.[25] Further, Daddy Grace claimed to be a messiah figure who stood in for God. He taught his followers that they could better achieve their goals through him than in praying to God directly.[26] Like Spiritualists and other ritually oriented groups, he encouraged the use of magico-religious activities among his followers for better health or good luck. Each House of Prayer sold the Grace brand of soaps, including face soap, hand soap and household cleansers, toothpaste, teas and coffees, hair pomades, powders, and even cookies. He claimed the ability to perform physical healings, even going so far as to promise cures for both the common cold and tuberculosis by placing the Grace magazine upon one's chest.[27]

Some of the prominent characteristics of the Pentecostal tradition are glossalalia, or speaking in tongues, an ecstatic worship style embodied by rhythmic music, dancing, hand clapping, an emphasis on the power of the Holy Spirit, and spiritual healing. The latter two characteristics, Spirit and divine healing, offer interesting points of overlap between New Thought and Pentecostalism.

Like Religious Science, the Pentecostal tradition places an important emphasis on the role of the Spirit. Both traditions maintain that Spirit is active in daily life and can be regarded as a healing principle. Pentecostals speak of the Holy Spirit in the traditional sense as the third person of the Christian trinity who can empower people at any time. The statement of belief of Church of God in Christ (COGIC), the leading Black Pentecostal denomination, reads:

> We believe that there is One God, eternally existent in three Persons: God the Father, God the Son, and God the Holy Spirit.

> We believe in the sanctifying power of the Holy Spirit, by whose indwelling, the Christian is enabled to live a Holy and separated life in this present world.[28]

On the other hand, Religious Science, like other New Thought groups, simply refers to Spirit as an indwelling manifestation of God that empowers a person from within and is always accessible. For example, the Religious Science Declaration of Principles states:

> We believe in the incarnation of the Spirit in all and that we are all incarnations of the One Spirit,"

> We believe that anyone may become a revealer of Truth who lives in close contact with the Indwelling God."[29]

In addition, the traditions share a belief in spiritual healing, perhaps their strongest connection. Pentecostalism
and New Thought share a historical origin in the late nineteenth century context in which Evangelism, Transcendentalism, American Spiritualism, and Mental Healing were all
coming into prominence. In a study of the roots of Pentecostalism as a healing and faith-cure movement, Raymond
Cunningham notes that even before the phenomenon of
speaking in tongues took precedence as a sign of sanctification, healing by faith was an earlier sign even within mainstream American evangelism.[30] As this practice diminished
in importance among mainstream denominations, the Ho-
liness-Pentecostal adherents maintained the healing directive as referenced in New Testament scripture. Particular
emphasis is given to the books of James, in which the laying
on of hands is prescribed for healing, and Mark, in which
healing is given as a directive to the apostles.[31]

The same scriptural foundations support the COGIC
belief in healing and its practice. The following statement
comes from COGIC's doctrinal teachings:

> The Church of God in Christ believes in and practices Di-
> vine Healing. It is a commandment of Jesus to the Apostles.
> Jesus affirms his teachings on healing by explaining to His
> disciples, who were to be Apostles, that healing the afflicted
> is by faith. Therefore, we believe that healing by faith in
> God has scriptural support and ordained authority...
> Healing is still practiced widely and frequently in the
> Church of God in Christ, and testimonies of healing in our
> Church testify to this fact.[32]

Likewise, Religious Science is a direct descendant of those
elements of the nineteenth-century religious atmosphere
that promoted New England Transcendentalism and Men-

tal Healing. The trajectory from that era to the founding of Religious Science in 1927 is full of healing testimonials, including those of the founders of Divine Science, Unity, and Christian Science.[33] Ernest Holmes maintained the magnitude of healing in his Religious Science teachings as noted in the Declaration of Principles, which states, "We believe in the healing of the sick through the power of this Mind."[34] (In this sense, Mind is an often-used term referring to God or the Universal Principle.) Religious Science teaches that the form of prayer known as Spiritual Mind Treatment is effective for healing any circumstance in one's life, including the healing of physical illness. In common practice, followers are encouraged to seek the help of one another and the lay leadership for "treatment." I have witnessed the testimonials of people claiming remission from diabetes, HIV/AIDS, as well as the healing of ailments formerly requiring invasive medical procedures.

Within their own individual systems, New Thought, Black Spiritual sects, and Black Pentecostalism all share beliefs in the power of the Indwelling Spirit to effect change in human life. As movements within African American communities, each addresses the particular needs and concerns of the people and reflect some of the characteristics commonly associated with African retentions. Religious Science and the Spiritualists share a thaumaturgical orientation, in which practitioners are personally active in shaping their lives; and Religious Science and Pentecostals such as the Church of God in Christ share a foundational belief in the importance of spiritual healing.

In the contemporary context we now see New Thought religious teachings merging with forms of evangelical and mainstream Christianity through the Word of Faith megachurches. These churches are led by charismatic ministers, usually male, who preach a gospel of prosperity to

largely African American congregations and television audiences. The influence of ministers such as Fred K. Price,
Creflo Dollar, Ed Montgomery, and Leroy Thompson Sr.
has become even more widespread through best-selling
books, talk-show appearances, and radio programs. These
ministries teach that the fruits of the Spirit will be experienced as spiritual growth and flowing abundance in all
areas of one's life.[35]

Fred K. Price is pastor of Ever Increasing Faith Ministries, which he established at Crenshaw Christian Center
in Los Angeles. The church is a 10,000-seat sanctuary on
the former campus of Pepperdine University. Price credits
his growth from three hundred members in 1973 as a result
of operating in faith and continually acting upon the
Word. He believes that the steady growth in church membership is a sign of faith. Price has stated that he wishes to
"reach his Black brethren with the Word of Faith and prosperity that is in Christ Jesus."[36] He wants to instruct Black
people in the ways of God that will point them toward their
own signs of increase.

Leroy Thompson Sr. is the pastor of Word of Life Christian Center, a member of Ever Increasing Word Ministries
in Darrow, Louisiana. His ministry is broadcast in syndica-
tion on various cable networks, including Black Entertainment Television (BET). Like his colleague Price, Thompson
teaches his congregation to break the bonds of poverty that
are unnatural to God's faithful people. He has published
books such as *I'll Never Be Broke Again, How to Find Your
Wealthy Place*, and *Money with a Mission*. He proclaims
that his mission is to teach people "how to live the life of
faith; how to walk by faith, not by sight; how to be well and
not sick; how to live and not die; how to keep the devil
under their feet; how to live the victorious abundant life in
Christ Jesus; and how to be led by the Spirit of God."[37]

Other independent ministries include Creflo Dollar and Ed Montgomery. Dollar leads a 20,000-member church called World Changers Church International from College Park, Georgia. Since 1986 he has been teaching his message of financial prosperity, and his ministry is now broadcast on the BET network as well. On a broadcast of March 2003, he acknowledged that other ministers often criticize him that his prosperity message is off course from the Christian message. He countered their criticism this way:

> The blood of Jesus was shed not only to deliver you from sin, but to deliver you from poverty, from living paycheck to paycheck, living in debt and living in the ghetto. Poverty is a curse.

> It is good news to the poor to hear that you don't have to be poor. Jesus has delivered you from the curse of poverty.[38]

Ed Montgomery, pastor of the Abundant Life Cathedral of Houston, also incorporates Christian prosperity teachings in his ministry. The community began in 1981 and now has six thousand members. His television ministry also airs on the BET network, where he is affirmed as "a twenty-first-century spiritual motivator." Many of his programs focus on bringing financial abundance to his congregation and to viewers, including the program of July 2002 entitled "The Blessing Factor," in which he proclaimed, "You need to be in a church that says you are blessed, you are prosperous."[39] He affirms that

> through the power of God, the community's outreach has led to salvations, physical and emotional healings, financial miracles and reuniting families. Their goal is "life overflowing: abundant life."[40]

These prominent African American ministers are lead-ing Christian megachurches that promote financial success as a part of God's plan for humanity. Reminiscent of Rev. Ike's style of ministry, each of these ministers has television ministries, appears in designer suits, and speaks about his own personal wealth as a manifestation of his faith. Like-wise, they teach their congregations that God is a prosper-ous God and that God's faithful followers are legitimate heirs to the wealth of creation. Consider Creflo Dollar's re-cently televised sermon series entitled "Releasing the Wealth Annointing."[41] In this program he encouraged the congregation constantly to affirm that "wealth is my inher-itance." Relying heavily on scriptures Deuteronomy 8:18ff and Genesis 15:4ff, he told them that "as a saved Christian, wealth is your right by covenant with God." Knowledge of this covenantal relationship empowers believers to expect wealth. He continued, "If you are begging God then you don't know your covenant and your rights and responsibil-ities under it."

While his sermons and those of his contemporaries are grounded in the Bible as the word of God and reflect the traditional Christological beliefs—that Jesus was God in-carnate and died for the redemption of humanity from sin —these ministers easily fall within the purview of the Black Gods of the Metropolis of sixty years ago. Within the con-texts of their more traditional Christian beliefs, they affirm the necessity for preaching prosperity and well-being to the poor and struggling classes. Both the mainstream Black churches and the newer urban sects have historically helped African Americans to creatively bypass the chal-lenges of disenfranchisement such as racism, segregation, poverty, and violence. In a number of ways, independent Black churches have always had to address racism and op-pression against African Americans whether they were sim-

ply upholding their humanity each week against a dehumanizing current, feeding the hungry, helping families set-
tle into new ways of life, or actively boycotting and picket-
ing against injustices. The current crop of Christian
megachurches focuses largely on economic empowerment
as their means of addressing disenfranchisement. Much
like the earlier ministries of Father Hurley and Father Divine, these contemporary churches see poverty as a major
oppressive force and seek to liberate their followers from
the limitations it imposes upon human wholeness. Rather
than fighting against the systemic causes of poverty and
other forms of oppression, these ministries seek to uplift
individual economic circumstances.

Rev. E followed a similar directive in her desire to take
Religious Science to Black communities in Oakland. After
completing a two-year ministerial internship at a predominantly White Religious Science church, she wanted to bring
New Thought to Black people because poverty is a way of
thinking that can be changed: "I wanted Black people to
know that Jesus spoke of an abundant life—they don't have
to be poor. I wanted Black people to have that."

The Christian megachurches are also similar to the New
Thought precursors in that they are not New Thought
churches, strictly speaking. They are churches that espouse
Christian theologies but have noticeably integrated New
Thought principles such as positive thinking, affirmation,
and prosperity into their mainstream teachings. For example, the statement, "All physical manifestation has its root
in the spiritual realm," could easily have been delivered by
Rev. E at the East Bay Church of Religious Science, but it
was in fact delivered by Creflo Dollar to his congregation at
World Changers International during an August 2003
broadcast. The lines are becoming blurred, and syncretism
is visible in many churches. This situation has not gone

unnoticed in some of the more traditional Christian sectors that have criticized ministries such as these.

For example, I witnessed a strong backlash from one of gospel music's most prominent singers, Yolonda Adams, while she was appearing on Ed Montgomery's program in February of 2001. She disdainfully stated that "we are on the verge of a New Age Christianity."[42] In her opinion, Christians who included practices of mysticism, yoga, or chanting in their spiritual lives were introducing demons into their consciousness. She went on to praise the leaders of the show on which she appeared, saying that she was confident that they would not allow that to happen at their church. She was obviously unaware of the New Thought sensibility that underlies the prosperity programs this same ministerial team teaches regularly.

At the East Bay Church of Religious Science, however, the merging of religious sensibilities and traditions has posed no problems. Many members of EBCRS see no conflict in maintaining affiliations with their former religious traditions. Consider the following comments from a few members: "Religious Science is my denomination of choice, but I still attend a Baptist church, too, because of my family ties."[43] "I like that New Thought is compatible with Christianity, Buddhism, and Islam. I can pick out those elements in it."[44] "I like Religious Science because it honors all people and denominations. Others are too narrow."[45] "I actually found Religious Science through Islam. Some of their literature was on a suggested reading list at the mosque I used to attend. Then my wife and daughter started coming to EBCRS, so I eventually did too."[46]

More and more, this type of syncretism is changing the way African American religion is defined. Churches like the East Bay Church of Religious Science are important to acknowledge because their worship expressions reveal the complexities of religious life and help us to reconsider what constitutes Black religion. They remind us that religious orthodoxy is more of an ideal than a practiced reality. Given the historical circumstances of African Americans who fashioned liberating religious experiences out of a mixed bag of African cultural retentions, Christianity, and the desire for freedom, it is no surprise that their religious expressions are likewise syncretistic.

3

Westward Migration
African American Communities in the San Francisco Bay Area

Get off in Oakland so you can make some con-
tacts. . . . The few Negroes around here in the Bay
District are in Oakland.[1]

California has been a very active center for New Thought religions. Like the Gold Rush before it, a health rush brought many people to California, who perceived the region as a healthier and less congested environment. The initial emphasis of New Thought was on physical healing. But as medical advances continued, New Thought groups began to shift the focus of their teachings to positive thinking that could be practically applied to all areas of life. By the 1920s California could easily be labeled "the metaphysical capital of the world," surpassing the number of followers in the East where the movement first caught fire.[2] California became a place for religious experimentation, drawing people who were searching beyond the boundaries of the established religions of the time. Ernest Holmes was one of those people, choosing to establish Religious Science in Los Angeles. This new religious milieu presented several viable alternatives to traditional Christianity, and many African Americans found these options to be spiritually compelling and began to seek them out.[3] Although they typically brought mainstream traditions with them from other regions, the atmosphere of cultural and religious diversity broadened the religious landscape for them.

Much of the California experience, or "frontier mentality" of carving out one's place in the world, is expressed in some of the comments from the congregation of the East Bay Church of Religious Science. People love the "freedom" they experience at the church. "When I think of EBCRS, I think of acceptance and diversity."[4] Consequently, those who attend do not feel pressured to conform to a particular type to fit in. "We have freedom of expression at EBCRS."[5] Moreover, as migrants or descendants of migrants, the members enjoy a sense of being able to create oneself outside of the social mores and expectations of more conservative regions of the United States. One member commented, "I moved to California because I felt a lack of freedom to be who I was [back East]. I felt I had to hide and therefore I felt isolated."[6] The members clearly appreciate the social and religious freedom they find at the church, yet they are also still able to embrace the familiar cultural elements that help them feel comfortable. EBCRS offers a mingling of new religious paths with familiar music, preaching style, and spontaneity. The East Bay Church of Religious Science is a place where diversities in class, sexual orientation, and religious backgrounds can meet.

California's historical development has been characterized by diversity, individualism, and spaciousness. Just as the northern migration made a significant impact on African American religious practices, so too would the westward migration shape African American religions in its own particular way. California represented a land of new opportunities for many ethnic groups including the Native American, Mexican, Chinese, and European. African

Americans were no exception. During the Gold Rush years (1840–1865), free Blacks came from the East hoping to explore business opportunities in the wide-open western frontier. Those who were slaves came forcibly with their masters until 1849, when the new state of California officially outlawed it.

African Americans imagined that more liberties would be available to them since they were not the primary targets of most of the active discrimination. The Native Americans and the Chinese, who made up larger segments of the population than Blacks, suffered the brunt of these indignities. While African Americans gained victories in the judicial system, such as the right to be recognized and the right to be compensated for discriminatory practices, California still denied them voting rights. The state repeatedly denied their appeals, and African Americans did not get their rights until the Fifteenth Amendment to the Constitution was passed in 1870 and remedied the situation nationally for Black males.

Religiously, northern California was characterized by the same sense of liberalism that typified the unstructured and untamed frontier ethos. Americans were flowing into the state chasing dreams of gold, land, and opportunity. By the time of California statehood in 1850, Protestant evangelicalism had become the moral guidepost for most of settled American society. However, traditional New England Protestantism with its Puritan work ethic and well-ordered social mores did not seem to lend itself to the California dream. By the 1870s, the mainstream denominational groups had begun to splinter into conservative and liberal factions presenting alternative visions of God and humanity from which believers felt they could freely select. Evangelicalism could only sustain itself in this diverse environment if it could adapt to the more tolerant attitudes of this new culture rather than attempting to set the cultural standard as it had done in the East. Traditional Protestants still faced challenges from liberal groups such as the Unitarians and metaphysical religions such as New Thought, Christian Science, and Theosophy, all of which were finding receptive audiences in the West. Each of these religions presented a perspective different from the traditional Protestant teaching of a sinful humanity redeemed only by faith in the atoning sacrifice of Jesus Christ.

One of the leading advocates of liberal religion in California was the Unitarian minister Thomas Starr King (1824–1864), principally associated with the First Unitarian Church of San Francisco. For almost four years he spoke throughout northern and central California, drawing people into an alternative religious perspective with his oratory skill and personal charisma. Arriving in San Francisco in 1861 to help the Unitarian church, he became a well-known speaker on matters of spirituality and politics. Though he always hoped to return to his New England home, he worked diligently in California affairs until his death in 1864. He preached an open and tolerant religious message and eschewed denominational boundaries. Starr King was well suited to the spiritual needs of California in the 1860s. Perhaps most importantly for the metaphysical religions that followed him was his often requested sermon on "Substance and Show," in which he stated that a spiritual reality lay behind all matter. He anticipated the metaphysical teaching that thoughts are things, later to be espoused by the New Thought movement. Indeed, he is remembered as being instrumental in the growth of liberal Christianity in California.

Through the efforts of people like Starr King, liberal Protestantism gained a small foothold throughout California. The ever-expanding religious and cultural environment included Unitarians, Universalists, Spiritualists, Seventh-Day Adventists, and New Thought religions. The old orthodoxy seemed antiquated and Puritanical, exactly the opposite of the new California identity which White Protestant Californians saw as expansive, open, progressive, and as pure and uncompromised as California's natural heritage.

The culture, influenced by Eastern Transcendentalism and Unitarianism, softened the teachings on sin and judgment and began to emphasize religious tolerance and independent thinking that transcended denominations. Metaphysical religions pressed the boundaries the furthest with a completely reworked anthropology and a nonanthropomorphic God who had been replaced by notions of a universal divine principle. Thus, a space was open in which alternative religious visions could emerge.

Such was the religious history and context into which African Americans in the Bay Area found themselves in the latter half of the nineteenth century. Their experiences, though different from their Anglo counterparts, were shaped (and often confined) by the political and religious structures that were taking shape.

African American Settlers Starting Again on Equal Ground, 1840–1930

Northern California began to grow during the 1860s with African American populations becoming concentrated in San Francisco, Sacramento, Marysville and Stockton, representing a large portion of the nearly five thousand Blacks throughout the state. They found that the most accommodating places to build their communities were in East Bay cities such as Oakland, Berkeley, and Richmond. By 1869,

Oakland was established as the final stop on the transcontinental railroad. In addition to being the largest employer of African Americans, the railroad port at Seventh Street became the nucleus around which a thriving African American business community grew, with retail shops, restaurants, and nightclubs. Southern-style restaurants, such as the late Sylvester Sims's Overland Café, boasted, "We serve well cooked home dishes from mustard greens to chicken dumplings, with corn bread and hot biscuits. Just like mother used to fix it."[7] The Seventh Street district thrived during these years.[8] "Oakland was the place to be for Blacks. And if you were lucky enough to get a job as a railroad porter, you were doing well."[9] The word spread that San Francisco was not as hospitable. A porter gave the following advice to a Black traveler:

> Get off in Oakland. There are not enough Negroes in San Francisco for you to find [them] in order to make some connections over there. Worst of all, you will never find a job. The few Negroes around here in the Bay District are in Oakland, so you can make some contacts.[10]

Black men found employment as tradesmen, barbers, or Pullman porters with the expansion of the railway. By 1929, one-third of all Black wage earners in Oakland were railroad employees.[11] Black women were mostly employed as domestics, though some found positions as teachers for Black children. There was a measure of stability in this environment, and African Americans began to create small community institutions such as churches, Masonic Lodges, schools, social clubs, and two newspapers, *The Pacific Appeal* and *The San Francisco Elevator*. The prominent churches were African Methodist Episcopal (AME) and Baptist. The AME church had the most members at first, but as the migrations from the South increased the Baptist churches expanded their influence. Shiloh AME Church (later renamed First AME) was Oakland's first Black congregation and was followed in 1889 by Beth Eden Baptist Church, which soon challenged the larger membership of Shiloh AME. Likewise, the following decade saw the rise of three more churches: Ebenezer Baptist, New Hope Baptist, and Cooper AME Zion.

The communities that developed in Oakland were modeled after White society, which was thought to lend legitimacy to African Americans as individuals and as a community. However, these parallel communities were not permitted to integrate. Thus, African American communities in the 1920s established many of their own political and social groups. The Oakland chapter of the NAACP had already been active when the Marcus Garvey movement came to Oakland in 1922. Many African Americans supported Garvey's nationalist political platform and the United Negro Improvement Association (UNIA), which he founded in New York, as an organization that promoted racial improvement and economic self-sufficiency. The Urban League also developed to fill a gap that the segregated YMCA and YWCA left in social services for Blacks. The various churches also provided space for political activism. Beth Eden Baptist Church, for example, was host to a UNIA spokesperson prior to Garvey's own Oakland visit. And A. Philip Randolph made a local appearance, speaking to a gathering at the Parks Chapel Church in West Oakland in 1926. Randolph had been instrumental in the unionization of Black Pullman porters by helping to form and lead the Brotherhood of Sleeping Car Porters, the first ever such union of Black employees.[12] Black women's organizations had become quite active in social and political organizations as well. One of their major conventions, the California State Convention of Women's Clubs, was held at the Fifteenth Street AME Church in 1930.

Both World Wars I and II offered a certain prosperity to African Americans in the East Bay with the increase of shipping and industry in the Oakland port. Historian James Noel reports that the number of Blacks employed in manufacturing and shipping jobs more than doubled during World War II, and that for the first time Blacks found employment in the aircraft industry.[13] In addition, Black people began to purchase homes and attained entry into some low-level civil service jobs. However, the Depression era between the wars was especially hard on them as they found themselves the first ones to be fired, suffering an unemployment rate many times greater than that of their White counterparts. Despite the Depression, another large migration of African Americans from the South and the Midwest to California occurred in the 1930s, but it was during and after World War II that the westward movement was greatest, with California receiving the highest numbers.[14] The great demand for factory workers encouraged many to leave their homes and make the journey in the name of seeking greener pastures. A common theme runs through the personal accounts of many who relocated to California.

I came from Arkansas where I used to be a beauty operator. My husband and me came out here because I had an uncle that lived out here and he told Booker that if he wanted to make more money and be more equal to come here. So he came first in '42, and I came in March of '43. I worked cleaning trains, worked at the Naval Air Station and eventually the shipyards where I learned to be a welder. There were a lot of women welders back then. The government needed everybody they could get to work.[15]

An account shared by one man about his grandparents provides another personal example:

> My grandparents came out from the south. My granddad from Alabama and my grandmom from Louisiana. They met at one of those little old juke joints down in the woods. My granddad told me that he used to work for 9, 10 or 11 cents a day plowing. They met up together, and when the recruiters came out to Louisiana to recruit Blacks to work in war plants, they got on the train and came out. They wanted to get out of Louisiana. My granddad didn't like the prejudice in Louisiana. He was what would have been called an uppity [Negro] back then. And in fact, I heard my grandmom say that he was lucky to get out of Louisiana, you know. So they left both for the opportunity in terms of employment and advancement that way, but then also because it was just too rigid back in Louisiana.[16]

This wave of migrations changed the dynamics of the population with a great influx of African Americans to the area. The Black population grew dramatically in Oakland from 1,026 in 1900 to 8,462 in 1940. Likewise, the San Francisco African American population grew from 1,654 in 1900 to 4,846 in 1940.[17] Racial tensions that had been under the surface began to rise as Whites in the area began actively to segregate themselves and refuse service to the ever-increasing African American population. Employment and housing discrimination became particularly pronounced at this time, leading to political activism in an effort to advance the case for equality.[18]

Meanwhile, the population in southern California began to grow as well. Initially, the earliest Black settlers had intermingled with Mexicans and led mostly agricultural lifestyles. Los Angeles became home to more African Americans after San Francisco's workers became unionized and the unions favored Whites. After World War II, the racial tensions that had plagued northern California became problematic in the south as well. Racial inequities surfaced in housing and employment, and police brutality rose against Blacks. African Americans in Los Angeles also began to experience ghettoization during the postwar economic downturn and as a result of White flight from various parts of the city. The Black areas were neglected in terms of public services and school funding. These tensions grew to a boiling point in the 1960s with the rise of the Black Panthers in Oakland and civil unrest in Watts.

African American Churches
Make Their Mark in Oakland

As civil rights issues began to take center stage in American life, African American churches took leadership roles in responding to the social crises at hand and in making a national call for justice. As we have seen, churches have always provided African Americans—as far back as the slave days —with a spiritual haven as well as a central location to vent frustrations and strategize for ways that could improve their situations. More specifically, the churches in the Bay Area from the early 1940s through the 1960s made their mark through the leadership of Oakland ministers such as the Reverends E. E. Hamilton, H. B. Gantt, Hamilton T. Boswell, F. D. Haynes, as well as Rev. Howard Thurman of the San Francisco–based Church for the Fellowship of all Peoples. All of them led important Black churches during this time and participated in the Black Ministerial Alliance that continually argued for equal employment, housing, and public services.[19]

Much of the information that is needed to contextualize the presence and social roles of African American churches still remains within the people and the churches themselves. As theologian Gayraud Wilmore has noted, "the history of many ordinary preachers, church members, congregations, and movements that began during the Great Migration and since, can only be reconstructed by means of the tape recorder."[20] I likewise found this to be the case, so I turned to local clergy and church members from the two most long-standing African American churches in Oakland—First African Methodist Episcopal Church (FAME) and Beth Eden Baptist Church—to help fill in the picture of Oakland's Black church communities.[21]

Many of these people shared their personal stories of migration, what it meant to them, and what they found when they reached California. During these discussions, those who had relocated to the state said they had done so in response to reports of plentiful employment opportunities, and due to stories heard through the grapevine that California offered a certain freedom from racial constraints. Most moved to the area as very young adults between the ages of sixteen and twenty-five, coming from Texas, Arkansas, Oklahoma, and Louisiana in search of work as railroad and shipyard workers, porters, schoolteachers, and cooks. In addition to finding jobs and housing, many considered it important to find a church home and intentionally looked for a suitable church in their new environs. Some wanted to maintain denominational ties while others were more concerned with convenient locations or the style of a particular preacher. These people had been longtime churchgoers in their home states, often belonging to the same church throughout their lives. A former railway porter from San Antonio, Texas, reported that even though he was usually away working most of the time, he still maintained his membership at the First AME Church in order to maintain community ties.

> I could always find out what was going on in Oakland from the church. There were a lot of prominent citizens at First AME, since it was the oldest Black church in Oakland, so whatever news there was, they had it.[22]

A former military man told me the story of his move from Louisiana to Washington with the armed services, then to northern California to join family who lived there:

> When I moved to California I needed to find me a church. I had always been a Missionary Baptist, so that's what I looked for. I ended up finding a church right here with the same name as my country church back home, Mt. Pisca Missionary Baptist church. So I went there.[23]

Mrs. Alice Williams, a former teacher and post office worker, told me more about the importance of denominational ties:

> I moved in 1940 with an aunt and uncle who came to work in the shipyards. I lived in San Francisco until 1957, then I moved to Oakland. I was raised AME, so we always went to Bethel AME since it was the only AME Church in San Francisco then. I kept going there even after I moved to Oakland. But I eventually found First AME over here, so I've been going there ever since.[24]

Clearly, churches provided a cohesive social setting during the post–World War II years for the many migrants who were joining the Oakland community. In the civil rights era of the 1960s, churches were often the central locations for organizing activities throughout the nation. Oakland churches had a particular role to play in light of the imminent presence of the Black Panther party. For example, St. Augustine Episcopal Church extended itself to the needs of the community as host of the Black Panther Free Breakfast Program for Schoolchildren, initiated in 1969. The relationship between the party and local churches reaffirmed the place of African American churches in the ongoing struggle for Black freedom and justice. Though this relationship could be strained, local churches lent support to the party in their efforts to develop free medical clinics, provide free food and clothing, and help the homeless find housing. They recognized that the organization filled a niche for some young people that churches did not.

With their quasi-military style, the Panthers presented a strong stance in the face of the inequitable status quo. They were able to rally the energy of young people into a force that brought the issues of housing, employment, education, and police brutality to the national front. Although their activities and methods were highly controversial, they provided important services to the Oakland community. For example, the Panthers were at the forefront of the resistance against the physical reconstruction that was going on in West Oakland, which caused many African Americans to lose their homes and businesses in the name of redevelopment.[25] Their first office space is an important highlight on historical tours of Oakland. This space continues to serve the community as a Black-owned business, providing jobs in its current incarnation, the It's All Good Bakery.

Form and Substance:
Old Church Roots and New Sensibilities

California history has shown that it can tolerate religious liberalism as well as new modes of ethnic expression. In addition to traditional Christian practices, African Americans have also participated in new forms of religious expression. Indicative of the nontraditional and revamped forms of expression within the state are two African American phenomena: Glide Memorial Methodist Church in San Francisco and the establishment of the Kwanzaa holiday by Maulana Karenga of California State College (now University), Long Beach.

The boundary-transcending ministry of Glide Memorial has grown successfully as a church that is strongly committed to the social justice directive of Methodism. The Reverend Cecil Williams led the church for over thirty years until his retirement in 2000. Under his pastorate the church became nationally known and acknowledged for its weekly celebrations and committed social services. In an economically disadvantaged area, Rev. Williams established a ministry that has bypassed barriers of class, race, gender, and sexual orientation. The church displays a radical form of Christian fellowship by embracing all those who have been marginalized not only by society in general but by other Christian churches as well. With regard to his vision for Glide, Williams has said, "The church is where you work out your stuff . . . a place where people could accept themselves and reject all ideas that they were non-persons."[26] As their members have become more middle class in their incomes and outlooks, many churches have not maintained a hands-on outreach and acceptance of the homeless, gay, lesbian, transgender, or bisexual person; the

person living with HIV/AIDS; or the drug addicted. With a radical vision, Glide provides a community space where the wealthy, the celebrities, the politicians all worship together alongside the poor, the unknown, and the uncared for. Glide Memorial has transcended the categories of Sunday morning segregation by liberally re-visioning the Christian gospel.

Maulena Karenga has brought a new ritual to African Americans. At least some of those now involved with Kwanzaa are Christians who could have never imagined that they might participate in a ritual that was not explicitly Christian. The fact that the ritual is now widely celebrated in most Black churches that claim some measure of Afrocentricity is a testament to the extent to which Karenga has legitimized an alternative religiocultural expression in his redevelopment of Kwanzaa. A first-fruits African celebration has been translated into an African American holiday practice of ritually affirming the African principles of community. It is celebrated during the traditionally sacred time of Christmas and Hanukkah. It offers a positive holiday ritual in which African American families and communities can participate away from the commercialism of the holiday season. Although this modern form of the ritual is a recent development, it has caught on and is annually celebrated throughout the United States and the African diaspora.

Both Kwanzaa and Glide Memorial reveal permutations in the religious expressions of African Americans. Glide Memorial is a United Methodist congregation, but it is unique in its radical embodiment of commensality that calls for the inclusion of the marginalized. Traditionally, African American churches have distanced themselves from matters of sexual orientation, and in so doing have alienated members of the community. Glide has created a

worship community that transcends this barrier. Its space consists of people from all walks of life "having church" together. Glide Memorial has transformed conventional, middle-class United Methodist polity into a model church community characterized by human complexities and intersections.

East Bay Church of Religious Science embodies these characteristics as well. It is a congregation where the "old church" comes together with a new doctrine, epitomizing California's spacious religious outlook. We have seen members' comments on the importance of social and religious acceptance, and that they believe the church is meeting that need. The people of EBCRS embody the transformation of religious identity by bringing together New Thought principles and African American worship aesthetics to create a religious experience that is liberating and fulfilling.

4

East Bay Church of Religious Science
in Perspective

"We're Almost Like Any Other Black Church"

The East Bay Church of Religious Science (EBCRS) offers many things to many people. It is a worship and meeting space where religious identities become transformed by the intermingling of religious sensibilities. Traditional aspects of African American worship are present, including rhythmic music, a Pentecostal-influenced sermon style, and an active call and response relationship between minister and congregation. However, these elements are brought together to support a kind of message that is different from what one might expect to find. Although there are familiar scriptures from the Bible, the Qur'an, and sometimes even the Bhagavad Gita, it soon becomes evident that New Thought is the primary teaching here. It is the structure upon which all other religious references are placed. The classic religions are taught parallel with the early twentieth-century writings of Religious Science founder Ernest Holmes. Those who attend are fashioning new religious identities for themselves.

EBCRS is a place where many have come in search of a new type of spirituality. For example, many of those I interviewed reported that they left their previous churches in search of something other than a sin and damnation message. "I would leave church feeling guilty all the time; I wanted something more positive."[1] "My old church was too controlling."[2] "This church is less judgmental than other churches."[3] "My old church did not feel right; it was restrictive, moralistic and emphasized sin."[4] Some members reported that they did not feel they were getting sufficient teaching and guidance elsewhere. They report seeking spiritual truth all their lives but not feeling satisfied until they found EBCRS. "I had been in church all my life, but I could never get answers to my questions, just fire and brimstone, nothing positive, which I found to be inconsistent with a loving God."[5] "I became dissatisfied with my church as I matured. I always had a quest for truth and to be at peace with myself. My therapist recommended EBCRS because she thought it would be compatible with my self-growth plan."[6] "Religious Science is a good fit; it teaches us to expect the answer, expect the miracles already."[7] "The minister's messages connect spirituality to reality, which I did not find in other churches."[8]

The spiritual quest was a recurring theme among interview participants. Members describe their association with Religious Science as finding spiritual food that empowers them and teaches them skills for improving their lives. EBCRS has been the focal point around which this community has transformed their ideas about religion, God, and themselves.

Community Profile

An important factor in the life of a church is its location. East Bay Church of Religious Science had been conducting services for over ten years in the heart of downtown

Oakland, two blocks from both the federal and state government buildings. The church's location in Preservation Park lent a serene atmosphere, creating a sort of liminal space between the activities on the city streets and the church sanctuary. The gated entrances into the park further suggested that visitors were entering a space set apart from the ordinary downtown activities of conducting business or shopping. This location had become a part of the identity of EBCRS; people who did not know the church well still knew about it through community word of mouth as "that church that meets in Preservation Park." However, in the spring of 2002 this changed when the congregation began to hold daily meditation services in the new church building located east of downtown at 4130 Telegraph Avenue. After members spent years searching for a suitable building to purchase, this property became available. The building had been used as a bar, a restaurant, and a small school and required numerous renovations before it was ready to be occupied as a church. The property consists of the former commercial space and an abandoned private home and lot purchased together. The church is currently using the commercial space while renovations continue on the house, which will be used for offices and meeting space. The church itself has been painted white and adorned with identifying signage in characteristic purple lettering.

The new neighborhood is a busy district of small businesses, characteristic of many urban areas, such as fast-food restaurants, bars, beauty supply stores, hair and nail salons, a car dealership, a body piercing and tattoo shop, several churches, and two mosques. The neighborhood becomes residential as one moves away from the commercial area.

The neighborhood and the church will undoubtedly have an effect on each other. For instance, the church will have much more immediate traffic, both pedestrian and automotive, since it is separated from the street only by a sidewalk. The gated garden atmosphere is no longer part of the EBCRS experience. Will this location bring people who may be curious about the church? Situated in the immediate vicinity of two Baptist churches, two mosques, and approximately a half-mile from the historic First AME church, the East Bay Church of Religious Science clearly stands out. Will the other churches welcome EBCRS to the community or will they be suspicious because it is different? These details remain for another study.

Besides the church's physical location in Oakland, we also need to understand its social location in the community it serves, the reputation and standing of the church, and the role it plays in community events, during crises, and so forth. It is critical to ask, with respect to the church's activities and number of ministries, whether these actions make an impact on the Oakland community in which it is located. The church's purpose statement clearly identifies itself as communally active:

> We, the East Bay Church of Religious Science, are dedicated to the spiritual transformation of the entire planet. We are committed to being a point of empowerment allowing Spirit to direct every thought, word, deed, and action for personal transformation. Our purpose is to serve as a spiritual development center by making available the knowledge and practice of the Science of Mind to all people by fostering their spiritual, cultural, and general well-being and to provide facilities of public worship, education and fellowship.[9]

The statement is prominently placed in the weekly church program and conveys the vision the church has for itself. The program lists twenty-eight ministries, activities, and outreach programs. Despite this number of ministries, I have observed that civil action is not a regular directive from the pulpit. Rather, the minister asks members to serve in ways that are insular to the church itself. For example, she asks volunteers to help with ushering, cooking, or working with the youth. These requests directly serve the needs of the church, not the outlying community. Although she does not discourage community involvement, it is noticeably not a common feature of her ministry.

One can look through the lens of the contemporary situation in Oakland to examine the church's self-perception of service to its community. At the time of this writing, Oakland is experiencing an alarming increase in street violence. According to local news reports during the first half of 2002, the homicide rate had already increased 28 percent over the same period the previous year.[10] By year's end, 120 people had become homicide victims. The violence has particularly affected the African American communities of North, East, and West Oakland. The response from City Hall has been an initiative to put more police into these communities, but residents have rejected the idea on the grounds that increased police presence is only a form of police occupation. The issues of poverty, poor schools, and limited opportunities are not being addressed. Residents accuse city officials of only wanting to suppress civil uprisings while burying their heads in the proverbial sand on the real issues that have led to the high rate of violent crimes in Oakland.

Churches such as Acts Full Gospel Church of God in Christ and Allen Temple Baptist Church are already known for their involvement in serving the communities most directly affected, and they are stepping forward to address this highly charged issue. On July 13, 2002, they joined a major rally held in downtown Oakland calling for action. Alongside the mayor and police chief, members of religious communities presented a strong front, some led processions from Allen Temple, St. Columba Catholic Church, and Mt. Zion Baptist Church. It is estimated that more than eighty churches, ministries, and community organizations were present before a crowd of about four thousand.[11] Many of the clergy believe the problem, although a complex one, is linked to the lack of youth involvement with churches and the churches' lack of involvement in the lives of youth. For example, Reverend George C. L. Cummings of Imani Community Church says that "churches have been woefully shortsighted. They have not responded [to the younger population]."[12] Dr. Bob Jackson, pastor of Acts Full Gospel, says that in the quest to be of service to people, "churches have lost their way and become social service agencies. Churches need to refocus . . . not making kids go to church . . . was the biggest mistake we ever could have made."[13]

While Rev. E has regularly participated in the Season for Nonviolence activities each April and has been recognized for her support of this event, her role in the community as an activist has been questioned by some East Bay Church of Religious Science congregants who would like the church to be more socially active, both locally and globally. The intensity of the situation in Oakland has brought many local clergy to take a public stand, but Rev. E's leadership has been noticeably absent from the current community outcry against violence. As one interview respondent commented, "Other churches are doing something to address issues of concern. East Bay should be a light, extend itself more, let people know they have a solution to offer people. Churches cannot be self-absorbed, but any church can be."[14] Another member notes that the church "does not act globally." He has been frustrated in his own attempts on some occasions to get the support of the minister and board members for his HIV/AIDS outreach programs. While church leaders have spoken in support of the work he does in Africa, he notes that the church has often acted slowly, but he has hope that the church will move forward. "As co-chair of this ministry I want to facilitate change."[15]

Although these members have been critical of the church in this area, both speak hopefully about the church's openness to growth. They expect the church to respond to the needs of the local community as well as the wider global village. In considering the church's responsiveness to community needs vis-à-vis the example provided by the current situation in Oakland, one must bear in mind the church's commitment to its own mission statement and the general Science of Mind principles. The first line of the mission statement reads, "We, the East Bay Church of Religious Science, are dedicated to the spiritual transformation of the entire planet." This may seem to be a clear indication that the church intends to be active in its community and work globally for change, and in some ways that is true.

Ernest Holmes taught that Religious Science is an individualized philosophy. The East Bay Church of Religious Science understands this to mean that the transformation of the planet occurs one individual at a time. Thus, Rev. E uses this directive to focus on the individual's life and circumstances, rather than on flaws in the social paradigm. During one of her sermons she addressed the local problem by saying, "To stop the violence in Oakland, I have to change the violent thoughts within me. Change happens on the inside."[16] In one of the Foundational Science of Mind classes, she replied to a theodicy type of question by saying, "I can't solve the problem of world suffering, but I can teach you how to raise your consciousness so that you do not suffer, and how you can hold a consciousness of wholeness for others. That's how we transform the world, by raising the consciousness of each person."[17]

Whether or not EBCRS exercises a social commitment ultimately comes down to a matter of internal consistency. Within the context of Religious Science philosophy, Rev. E leads the church toward social responsibility one individual at a time. Her admonition to each person to keep his or her consciousness on the wholeness and perfection of God reflects the Science of Mind orientation. The philosophy teaches that planetary transformation happens at the individual level. "We can uplift the planet starting right here. Just clean up your own heart and it will have a ripple effect."[18]

It may appear that this religion makes no effort toward community involvement, but this conclusion would not adequately recognize the value that Religious Scientists place on the power of prayer and meditation to transform the world. In this system, consciousness is everything; thoughts are things and have the power to set events in motion. The church's purpose statement reflects a more passive position by offering itself as a spiritual development center where all are welcome to participate in worship, education, and fellowship according to Science of Mind principles. Thus, EBCRS's self-concept that it is a community concerned with transforming the planet is internally consistent but leaves itself open to the criticism that the church has fallen short in the face of local crisis and may look like a church that remains an island unto itself.

Church Organization

The institutional aspects of Religious Science are exemplified by two organizations, the United Church of Religious

Science (UCRS) and Religious Science International (RSI). The organizational split between the two groups occurred in 1953 as a result of disputes among member churches over issues of centralized authority. Church leaders who disagreed with the emerging trend toward centralization left the Church of Religious Science (later renamed United Church of Religious Science) and established RSI, where they felt greater individual freedom.[19]

The East Bay Church of Religious Science belongs to the United Church of Religious Science (UCRS), headquartered in Los Angeles. EBCRS is currently participating in the UCRS Organizational Renewal Project, which is designed to reorganize many of the current structures and operating procedures. While participating churches still maintain their operational autonomy, they are considered part of a network of 225 churches and study groups that adhere to a set of bylaws and a community covenant agreement established by the "home office." The covenant agreement includes "conscious alignment with the Science of Mind teachings as stated by Ernest Holmes, the shared values and shared vision of the United Church of Religious Science, and the guiding principles stated in the Organizational Design Model are the minimal requirements for affiliation and participation in the Community."[20] The agreement also contains other points in which a member church may elect to participate, such as tithing into a community pool and mentoring developing churches.

East Bay Church of Religious Science operates as a member of this network of churches, but at the individual church level it operates independently under the leadership of its minister and Board of Trustees. Board members are elected for three-year terms with the exception of Rev. E, who is a nonrotating member. The major decisions that will affect the church, such as financial expenditures, acceptance of new Practitioners, or the recent relocation to a new facility, are discussed and voted upon by the board. They are the "stewards of business." Rev. E made an exception to the usual process recently when she announced that she had decided to purchase a baby grand piano for the new sanctuary. She said that since she had "gone out on a limb," she would "look to the generosity of the congregation to help out." As it turned out, two generous members donated large sums to pay for the down payment.

I learned from interview subjects that this type of decision making happens more frequently than one might suppose. The arrangement of checks and balances between the board and the minister sometimes falters, as might happen in any institution. One subject shared that "some boards are better than others. Some people, when they come in, have more fear and don't want to make any moves, but the bottom line is that things still get done the way they are supposed to. It's all God, so it's all good."[21]

Another major part of the operating structure at EBCRS is the corps of fifty-five Practitioners. With this growing number, the locus of power is expanding to include their voices. A Practitioner told me that "leadership is shared more than it was five years ago."[22] This group of men and women are the lay leaders who lead outreach and ministry programs, coteach classes, and offer spiritual support to the congregation through one-on-one treatment and counseling. Many wear multiple hats of responsibility within the church, and some attend the ministerial school, the Holmes Institute, at the home office in Los Angeles. The Practitioner told me that he felt that Rev. E. is a great leader because of her ability to teach and mentor other great leaders. He feels that "she is developing a lot of spiritual leadership under her wing. She will probably become known for that. She builds other leaders."[23]

Minister Profile

The Reverend Doctor Elouise Oliver, known affectionately as Rev. E to the church community, was born Elouise Dixon on April Fool's Day, 1932, in the rural town of Munson, Florida. She married her childhood sweetheart, William Oliver, at fifteen. He joined the army and they began moving around together while starting their family. They had seven children, most of whom take an active role at EBCRS. One son leads his own Religious Science church in San Francisco. Life was challenging for the young couple and William developed a drinking problem. Rev. E, known at that time as Candy, did what she could to provide for the family and keep it together. She was on welfare for a time, but studied nursing and was able to contribute to her family as a nurse.

Rev. E. credits her upbringing in the rural South, which she terms "the country," with her current status. Her experiences and now her ministry have been informed by life "in the country" without technological advances or even modern medical care. She says these things allowed her to see healing through the laying on of hands, the administering of wild plants, and the belief that there is a greater power who is the real healer one relies on. She remembers that her grandmother "would respond to the negative reports of the country doctors with 'the devil is a liar.' They would make up a pot of collard greens and use the [pot] liquor for medicine. They knew all healing comes from God."[24] Rev. E often shares her own story of being healed through prayer. She once suffered from chronic asthma and ulcers, but through the prayers of a group of "prayin' women" she fully recovered from what she believed to be a terminal asthma attack and never suffered from these attacks again. She interweaves many of her own life experiences into her sermons, making them real for the listeners. One Sunday, after she was asked how she increased church membership from thirty to over one thousand, she answered that she just tells her story. She believes that through telling her story in a transformative way, "somebody can be healed."[25] Thus, her hermeneutic is informed by the Christianity and folk expressions of her parents and grandparents. As womanist writers and theologians have taught, there is value to understanding God through the social and cultural location of African American women.

Much of Rev. E.'s religious sensibility has been shaped by her Pentecostal history. She recalled her grandmother's interpretation of scripture from childhood, when she was immersed in church life, and continued her Pentecostal beliefs as she became an adult. Her family first settled in San Francisco, then Berkeley, where she and her children became members of Ephesian Church of God in Christ. However, when she was introduced to New Thought through her mother-in-law's affiliation with Unity, she started in a new theological direction. Rev. E says that she had no trouble accepting New Thought teachings because at the core of it all, "I recognize that everybody is teaching the same thing."[26] Further, she admits that she had been dissatisfied with the Pentecostal church over the years because of the sexism that kept women out of the pulpit. She recalls her frustration as a child when her brothers were allowed to participate in certain parts of the services and she was not because she was a girl. She was bothered even then by the contradiction between the minister's regular reference to God as no respecter of persons and the practice of limiting women's contributions in church. She says she "just knew God could not be a God of preferences."[27]

When her mother-in-law began inviting her to the Unity church in Oakland in 1970, she admits that she often fell asleep because of her night-shift hours as a nurse. Yet her mother-in-law urged her to keep coming because the unconscious mind would absorb the teachings even in sleep and benefit her nonetheless. Rev. E. was amenable to this suggestion, because she already appreciated certain aesthetics of the church, such as the fact that this church had a female minister. In addition, she liked the quiet, meditative atmosphere and the stained glass artwork that featured a Black Jesus.[28] She was eventually introduced to Religious Science by attending a lecture at the First Church of Religious Science in Oakland. While the doctrine resonated with her, she simultaneously continued her relationship with Ephesian Church of God in Christ. She found that following the brief one-hour services at First Church, she did not "feel like she had had church."[29] First Church had no gospel music, and only the occasional soloist would perform. So she would leave and go to Ephesian, where she knew "they would still be having church with some gospel music."[30] Her association with First Church lasted four to six years, during which time she became a Religious Science Practitioner and began attending ministerial school in San Jose. She served as an assistant minister there before leaving in 1974 to join the founding minister of East Bay Church of Religious Science, Dr. Earl Evans.

At that time the church was an all-White congregation that met on Fruitvale Avenue at the Masonic Temple. When Dr. Evans retired, there was a succession of five other ministers before Rev. E assumed leadership. The church membership had dropped to just thirty-seven, and the community had received word from the home office of the United Church of Religious Science in Los Angeles that they should consider operating as a study group instead, a designation for groups of fifty or less. However, Rev. E accepted the leadership of the church and decided not to assume study group status. She felt that things couldn't possibly be worse with the church and that the opportunity had come to her for a reason. As she says, "The rest is history." The membership grew, necessitating a new facility. She led them to Preservation Park, where they remained for many years, until again outgrowing their space and moving into their own building in 2002.

While she values the Religious Science philosophy and her ministerial position in the church, Rev. E acknowledges that she is still connected to her Pentecostal roots. In response to the question whether or not this sensibility influences her current ministry, she simply stated, "Yes it does, it's who I am. Religious Science just added to what I already had from the Bible. It [the Bible] is what has given me strength." For example, she continued, "I came [to New Thought] for the philosophy, but then I would go back to Ephesian so I could get me some church. So I decided at East Bay we would have gospel music."[31] Furthermore,

> If not for the sexism of the Pentecostal church I may have remained, because I don't see a lot of difference. God is one. It's just they talk about heaven and hell, good and evil, we talk about actions and consequences. They focus on a wrathful God, we say God is no respecter of persons, and will do for any and all what he does for anyone. People don't realize that the Science of Mind textbook teaches the same thing that the Bible teaches.[32]

Regarding her leadership of East Bay Church of Religious Science, she says "I teach that Religious Science is about raising consciousness and understanding that our thoughts are the consequence of our consciousness."[33]

Member Profiles

The membership of East Bay Church of Religious Science presents a diverse demographic profile. People come from a variety of socioeconomic, geographic, and denominational backgrounds. While the church is by far mostly African American in population, there is a steady population of other races including White, Latino, and biracial people. In addition, there is a relatively large openly gay and bisexual community within the church. In the course of my field-work, I have formally interviewed twenty people from the church and spoken to many others through informal conversation. I interviewed nine women and eleven men, ranging in ages from twenty-six to seventy-two, with the highest concentration falling into the twenty-six to thirty-five year range. Seventeen participants out of twenty are transplants from the East or the Midwest, and three of the older participants (over age sixty) migrated from the South. In addition, income levels among those who chose to reveal their earnings ranged from $26,000 to over $90,000, with the highest concentration falling between $66,000 and $75,000. According to a 2002 census report, the median income for Oakland was $62,877 giving the church a middle to upper middle class orientation.[34]

In his study of a Pentecostal church in Pittsburgh, Melvin Williams identifies church members according to their roles and relationships within the church community. He identified elite, core, supportive, and marginal categories in which to explore issues of status, personality dynamics, levels of commitment, self-perceptions, and effective management.[35] As I attempt to represent the human component of the East Bay Church of Religious Science, I find these categories to be useful as well.

First, Williams describes the elite group as individuals who are articulate, ambitious, and capable of manipulating the mechanisms of mobility. They raise the most money, plan activities, and lend constant support and loyalty to the pastor. They have immediate access to the pastor and get maximum exposure within the church. Everyone knows who they are. Second, Williams describes the core members. They carry out the plans of the elite, providing the services that keep the church running—ushers, nurses, kitchen staff, cleaning people, choir, ministers, and so on. They receive limited but notable exposure within the church, usually in the form of praise for their service. The supportive group is made up of those whose lives are not integrated into the church; they do not participate in church dynamics; they do not provide substantial amounts of time or money; they enjoy the church but do not seek status or validation from it. Finally, Williams describes the marginal group, which consists of individuals who are ineffectual for service or significant contribution due to handicap or behavior problems. He also uses this category to refer to "backsliders" and those whose attendance is unpredictable.[36] What follows is a representation of what these designations look like in the context of the East Bay Church of Religious Science.

At EBCRS the elite designation corresponds to the "inner circle," those closest to Rev. E. This circle includes Rev. E's adult children who have positions within the church, the Board of Directors, the senior-level Practitioners (who have held that position the longest) and guest speakers.

Cheryl Tucker has been a Practitioner for seven years.[37] Now in her fifties, she has risen to the realm of lay leader, workshop facilitator, author, and occasional minister within the church. When she came to the church she had been through a turbulent marriage, severed family relationships, and attempted suicide. However, at EBCRS she found the knowledge and wisdom to regain her self-esteem and the ability to rebuild her life. She frequently refers to her current marriage as a "gift" and to her husband as "the love of my life." Cheryl acknowledges that she has become a new person due to her understanding of herself, to the teachings of Religious Science, and to the mentoring of Rev. E. She says, "I have a great teacher and role model in Rev. E. She shares so much of herself—her own story, her life, and her time."[38]

Even the observer is made aware of their close relationship because they often refer to each other during services; they pray together and make plans together. On many occasions they have shared the pulpit on Sundays or alternated the three services in order to give Rev. E a rest from preaching at all three. Currently, Cheryl is attending ministerial school to further pursue her own calling.

The core group at EBCRS consists of those Practitioners who are not among the elite, the leaders who run the auxiliary or sacred service ministries, and the volunteers who help in whatever capacities they are needed. To recognize the ongoing contributions of the volunteers, the church sponsors an annual Volunteer Brunch. Some core members achieve recognition and limited exposure through this event. Others may be recognized for special service to the church or asked to give personal testimony regarding a particularly successful experience. Rev. E generously acknowledges the critical functions consistently performed by members of this group. Also, as Williams noted, at least some of the members of the core group want to rise into the elite and strive for recognition from the minister.

Raymond Luke could be characterized as a volunteer's volunteer.[39] He is involved in so many aspects of the church that it is hard to imagine a Sunday without his presence. He sings in the choir, participates in the men's groups, volunteers anytime there is a need to move furniture or clean up, and willingly fills in for others who may need a break from their own duties. In his early fifties, he has experienced underemployment and unfulfilling relationships in the past. Despite these challenges he maintains a cheerful, welcoming attitude each week. When I have asked him how he is doing, Raymond always responds, "Oh, I'm blessed. God sees to that. If I have any of my own stuff come up, I know to just get out of the way."[40]

Raymond's face and voice are familiar to everyone, and it is clear that he helps to get things done around the church. Some Sundays at Preservation Park, when the room would have to be cleared out quickly after use, Rev. E would conclude her announcements by calling for people to "help Raymond move these chairs outta here." While there are many others who volunteer a good deal, he clearly receives a lot of recognition for his efforts. However, it is not clear to me that he aspires to join the ranks of the elite. Although he takes the classes and participates at the church, he does not overtly place himself in leadership capacities. Raymond appears to be happy with his role at the church, perhaps knowing that people appreciate his dependability.

Those who fall into the supportive group at EBCRS are harder to identify because by definition they resist participating in any church groups. These individuals come for service only and leave without much social interaction. They may be known "by face" because of regular attendance, but no one knows much about their personal lives. The supportive members do not volunteer or attend special functions, nor do they seek status in the church. They are content participating from a distance.

Sylvia Johnson is in her late thirties and has been attending EBCRS for about two years.[41] She came to the church while seeking an alternative to the messages of sin and guilt she was getting from the traditional Christian churches she had attended throughout her life. She says she was "tired of feeling bad about herself" and enjoys the positive environment of her new church. Sylvia's lifestyle is busy with her career, travel, community activities, and helping out with her extended family. While she is a regular attendee, she does not come to church every Sunday. Her routine is to come when she can and take the positive message with her as she attends to the rest of her activities. Sylvia likes to attend a convenient, regular church, but she also likes the freedom to come and go at will, and so she does not get very involved in other activities at the church. My observations and conversations with her confirm that her life is full and she gets a lot of validation from her profession and from her personal relationships. EBCRS is a positive addition to that life.

Williams described marginal members as "backsliders" or people who are incapable of giving much support to the church due to a physical or mental handicap.[42] I would reinterpret that description for EBCRS to refer to those who are relatively unknown due to their sporadic attendance. People in this group make no contribution to the church because they are rarely present, perhaps having more demanding responsibilities elsewhere. Joe Brown and Rita Smith fit into this category.[43]

Joe is in his late thirties and considers himself a spiritual seeker on a path to discover his true calling and to bring it forth. He is an avid student of religious truths, and therefore finds himself pulled in many directions. Joe's intellectual grounding is in Religious Science, but his emotional needs led him to one of the local Pentecostal churches where he spends most of his Sundays. He told me, "I just let Spirit tell me each Sunday morning where to go." He has many professional and spiritual goals for himself and relies upon self-actualization teachings to bring them about. For him, EBCRS is a place to get good teaching and inspiration, but he believes he can get that from his own reading of Science of Mind literature; therefore, he attends the church only on occasion.

Rita Smith is in her late twenties and is self-employed. She does not regularly attend any church. She says, "I go to East Bay Church if I want to hear something positive, but if I want to hear a more Christian sermon I go somewhere else or I just don't go anywhere."[44] For her, going to church is a special occasion that she enjoys, but not enough to be a member of any one institution. Because she has her own shop she often works on Sundays, not allowing her to be at church every week. When I asked if she liked the church, she replied, "I like East Bay, but I just can't say I'm going to come all the time."[45]

While Melvin Williams's terminology is somewhat arbitrary, it is helpful for discovering the layers that exist within church membership, even within a church like EBCRS that claims an egalitarian membership from the top down. Although it was not my intention here, a categorical review like this can also be helpful for revealing that individual agendas exist, and perhaps even shed light upon internal conflict and its resolution.

Religious Science in Cultural Context

In addition to getting to know East Bay Church through the characteristics of its members, I give a wider view of the church milieu by presenting some of the church activities in their African American cultural context. Therefore, I paid special attention to those who told me why they returned to the church and what they enjoyed most about it. I found that a pattern emerged from their responses: style and content of sermons, performed aspects of African American cultural elements, and cultural politics of difference embodied by the congregation.

I established the first category, sermon content and style, because many people commended Rev. E's sermons. While the congregants appreciate the personal empowerment boost they receive from the general Science of Mind message, most of the respondents also claimed to resonate with her "down to earth" manner and her real-life experiences that frame the content of her sermons. The most frequent comment from respondents was that they can relate to her stories. As noted earlier, her sermons are infused with Southern culture, making connections between what she learned from her grandparents' religion and what Religious Science teaches. Her goal is always to reinforce the principle of oneness no matter what the particular religious manifestation is. Two interview respondents referred to her integration of old-time religion. One stated, "I haven't heard other New Thought teachers speak they way she does, integrating old-time religion through her own experiences."[46] Similarly, the other commented, "Rev. E pulls from her background of down-home religion and old-time style."[47]

However, Rev. E has made a noticeable change in the content of her sermons by substantially increasing her use of the Bible. During my fieldwork I became aware that Bible teaching had become a more frequent request from at least a large enough portion of the congregation for Rev. E to address it. Her response had always been that the Science of Mind textbook and the Bible teach the same thing (except sin and damnation), but since the request had been made she happily agreed to be more intentional about making these connections. Her remarks had generally made a reference such as "the scripture says . . . ," but now she gives a specific chapter and verse notation, cross-referencing it with the Science of Mind textbook.

In response to this shift in content, I began to ask interview subjects how they felt about her inclusion of biblical text in Religious Science sermons. One person commented that the criticism against Rev. E had been unfair, stating that "Religious Science is what it is, if people want more Bible teaching they should go somewhere else for it."[48] Others praised Rev. E for the more deliberate inclusion of biblical scripture. "I'm so happy she got back to it; I think she didn't know if the congregation would accept it, but it's what a lot of people know."[49] "I love the inclusion of scripture; it helps her give the philosophy her special touch."[50] "Her inclusion of scripture is great. I get a new interpretation of the scriptures. The traditions say the same thing but our interpretation is different than theirs."[51]

Embodied spirituality is also present and valued at East Bay Church. I refer to this observable embodiment as performance in the sense that there are behaviors and customs among the group that seem to be normative. For example, at any given Sunday service, it is customary to see spontaneous dancing and people jumping up from their seats, waving hands, swaying bodies, and verbally exhorting the minister to "Preach!" These events might occur during the sermon, while the choir is singing, or, less frequently, during prayer.

In addition, the choir also contributes to this performance of an African American cultural and religious aesthetic. One person commented, "A choir has to have soul, this one has it."[52] It is indeed a gospel choir, regularly performing reworked gospel standards, such as "Gonna lay down my burden"; contemporary R&B music from Michael Jackson, R. Kelly, and the Isley Brothers; Negro spirituals; and various Psalms. For example, one popular song the EBCRS choir performs is an adaptation of Psalm 121, "My help comes from the Lord." It is one of the few songs in which the choir director, Michelle, sings the lead, which is also part of the reason that the song is so well loved among the congregants. Michelle is considered by the church to be an exceptional singer, although she usually places other singers in the soloist position. On one occasion Michelle was asked by a visiting minister, Brother Tetteh from Ghana, to perform this song. Although the choir was not scheduled to sing it and they had in fact finished singing for this service, Brother Tetteh asked if Michelle would do him the personal favor of singing this song. He had remembered it from his last visit, several months before, and had loved it so much that he wanted to hear it again. She agreed, and began to sing slowly and quietly:

> I will lift up my eyes to the hills from
> which cometh my help,
> my help cometh from the Lord
> the Lord who made heaven and earth . . .
> The Lord who said, I will not suffer thy
> Foot, thy foot to be moved,
> The lord who never slumbers nor sleeps
> the lord who keepeth thee . . .

While the congregation always responds positively to the choir each week, on some occasions the effect is visibly different. Whenever Michelle sings this song, the congregants are rapt, they sing along, they move slowly from side to side, and they cry. For some the tears run down their cheeks profusely, for others it is only noticeable because they dab at their eyes with tissues. The ushers move quickly through the aisles with boxes of tissues, unlike their usual slow stroll up and down the aisles. This time was no exception; it seemed that everyone was in tears, moved deeply by the words of the song and Michelle's delivery of them. The performative aspect is that which can be seen, but the song clearly touches upon something unseen as well, perhaps corresponding with an intense and visceral connection with the divine. The song opens the believer's consciousness to a faith validating experience that all is well.

Similarly, I have observed style of dress as a performed element of identity. As a common marker of identity, clothing is often used to convey information about the wearer. At EBCRS it is common for churchgoers to wear African-inspired clothing. Rev. E is known to wear African dresses, robes, and headdresses almost every Sunday. Further, the various choir groups often choose African wear as their clothing theme. This means of displaying an African identity suggests to me the desire on the part of the churchgoers to maintain a cultural focal point as African Americans. Along this line I was told, "At East Bay we are African inspired, but Americanized."[53] Also, "We like to exhibit our Black culture here."[54] "We're almost like any other Black church."[55]

There are exceptions to the normativity aspect. One Sunday I witnessed an impressive service outside the behavioral norm. It was nonetheless important to note as a unique event because the cultural context of the church had already laid the groundwork to allow this atypical performance to happen there.[56] In addition, it offers critical supporting evidence for my position that EBCRS embodies an African American Pentecostal worship aesthetic, making it a unique Religious Science congregation.

The service of April 21, 2002, went as follows: Rev. E was away for the week and asked Rev. Ahman, who at one time had been a minister of East Bay Church, to step in for her. Rev. Ahman delivered a sermon entitled "The Prayer of Faith." He began by making reference to the power of the Holy Spirit and the importance of faith for demonstrating or manifesting one's desires. Referring to passages from the Bible, he affirmed that all human beings are God incarnate and have the ability to move mountains or curse the barren fig tree through the power of their word and faith in God, as Jesus has done.

Throughout his sermon he relied upon scriptures from the books of Mark and James to build a foundation for affirming and practicing spiritual healing. Rev. Ahman wanted to reinforce the idea of the power of a faith community comprised of two or more gathered in the name of God to accomplish whatever they would. What I found really remarkable about this service (and very surprising to the congregation) was the deliverance of this service in a style that Rev. E commonly refers to as "the old church." Whereas she often refers to sayings and practices of the old church, Rev. Ahman actually took the group back to that old church and led it to enact a laying-on-of-hands healing prayer ritual. The congregation was asked to gather around him in the center aisle, forming a free-form circle, and he began to lead a prayer that was a version of "speaking in tongues." In using this term, he explained that "for us (religious science practitioners) this means turning over our will and our tongues and voices to God, allowing God to take over and say whatever it will through us." He then led the prayer by encouraging the group to offer up praises such as "Hallelujah" or "Praise the Lord" or whatever they felt was appropriate. As people joined in, the room became filled with voices reciting their own prayers for their own benefit and those of others. The jumble of voices emerged as a "foreign tongue" to anyone trying to make sense of any one prayer. Rev. Ahman continued in the center, his voice slightly louder than the group voices. He encouraged people to curse the things that no longer served them (as Jesus had cursed the barren fig tree), and to create the things and experiences they wanted through believing and knowing that their words were "power unto the law of God and would bear fruit." He encouraged all to pray for one another without worrying about knowing the needs of the next person, but relying upon the Spirit to guide them for that person's benefit.

This experience went on for about ten minutes, after which people shouted "Amen" and "And so it is!" while returning to their seats. The end of the service proceeded as usual with collections, recognition of visitors, and the benediction. Rev. Ahman had enacted a participatory event among a congregation that was accustomed to the inward path or the mental exercise. While the members of EBCRS are used to lively music and spontaneous events like dancing or waving of their hands, or call and response with the minister, this event went far beyond anything I had observed at the church over my five-year affiliation with it. Rev. Ahman inspired the congregation to a *performed* ritual of healing reminiscent of the Pentecostal tradition, in that he invoked the language (speaking in tongues) and the healing concept (laying on of hands) associated with that tradition to support his sermon.

The response from the congregation during the ritual was positive, and most of the people in attendance rushed to the center of the room when Rev. Ahman called for it, but afterwards I heard a variety of comments. In an informal manner I began asking people what they thought about the service, and where I could inconspicuously hear people's conversations, I heard responses such as "Well, that was different" and "That was a bit too much," as well as "Wow, I really felt the Holy Spirit moving in there." The following week I asked different people what they thought about the previous week's service, and I received many more of the "that was different" kind of comment, said in a way that I perceived as somewhat disapproving because it was often mumbled and mixed with a raised eyebrow. I have attended previous services that Rev. Ahman had led in Rev. E's absence, and I have noted a positive response to his lively, energetic delivery; but on this occasion it seemed that at least some people felt somewhat overwhelmed.

What these reactions suggest to me is that Rev. E manages to maintain a more delicate balance between the African American Pentecostalism of her background and the inner path of Religious Science that she later adopted. Perhaps because it is her home congregation, she intuits how much "old church" might be received as uplifting and how much might be received as too much. Rev. Ahman's ritual and the congregation's reaction to it reinforce the importance of intersecting phenomena for this church. The worship sensibilities of this group reflect a hybridization of more traditional practices from both Pentecostalism and Religious Science. Even though there is a cultural context for this type of event at the church, it would appear that the churchgoers already receive and appreciate a specific mixture, delivered in a way that maintains their comfort level.

Sermon style and performance clearly demonstrate the presence of the traditional elements of the African American cultural and religious aesthetics. Together, they affirm the importance of culturally familiar music, preaching style, and congregational performance needed for the success of this church. The third category, the cultural politics of difference, speaks to my point that EBCRS represents a mode of religion different from what has been traditionally noted on the spectrum of African American religiosity. We have already seen how the Religious Science teachings of the church differ from those of traditional African American Christianity; this category further demonstrates the multiplicity of differences that coexist at EBCRS.

The cultural politics of difference that exists at East Bay Church manifests in both demographics and religious syncretism. The church body reflects widely across the spectrum of human activity. There are laborers, service industry workers, trades people, artists, lawyers, health-care workers, computer specialists, educators, administrators, politicians, and entrepreneurs. I interviewed some people who were unemployed and some who earned six-figure incomes. Some people attend church in jeans and T-shirts; others wear suits or dresses with matching hats and shoes. Some drive pickup trucks, some drive upscale SUVs or Mercedes-Benzes. The church honors the commitments of gay and straight couples alike. They welcome the elderly, the handicapped, and the wailing infant. They encourage the recovering addict, the ex-con, the "street person," and the HIV/AIDS patient.

There seems to be a good deal of pride placed in the way the church community embraces all people from whatever station in life they may come. Many respondents note the ease of being themselves in the community, not feeling judged by appearances. "East Bay is very welcoming and unpretentious."[57] "People come here from all walks of life; it's the teachings and the atmosphere that make it a good place to be."[58] "It's special because the atmosphere is so relaxed, no putting on airs. I just try to see others as an expression of God no matter who they are."[59] The latter comment sums up the sentiment that Rev. E often declares, that

God is not a respecter of persons, therefore regardless of circumstances each individual is considered to be whole, perfect, and complete. I have observed this cross section of people and have often not been able to determine individual economic or class standing. I have observed the attendance of celebrities and politicians who come just to hear the message. While no one church can be all things to all people, East Bay Church of Religious Science does offer a diverse demographic climate, and even appears to have a small but stable body of non-Black attendees. The racial diversity includes biracial people, Whites, Hispanics, and a few Asians. This diversity led one interview respondent to say, "Well this *is* the Bay Area; no telling what we will look like in five years."[60]

Furthermore, the religious syncretism present at EBCRS contributes substantially to a cultural politics of difference that recognizes contemporary people have multiple influences on their lives. Because many Religious Science teachings are compatible with other faith traditions, many East Bay churchgoers are happily eclectic in their religious practices. Most of my interview respondents came from traditional Christian churches such as Baptist, Methodist, Episcopalian, and Roman Catholic; one came from Christian Science and another from the Unity School of Christianity. All of them noted that they felt free at East Bay to stay in touch with those roots as they wished. One respondent told me that he occasionally visited his former United Methodist church because of family ties. Another frequently referred to Jesus during our interview session, so I asked her if she considered herself a Christian. She replied that she would always consider Jesus to be God. "Jesus makes God more accessible to me. I guess I will always be Baptist to some degree."[61] Another person commented, "I like Religious Science teachings and I can identify other

traditions with it."[62] Still another, "I identify as Episcopalian, but practice Religious Science because I wanted
something more positive." In another interview I was told,
"I don't want to give up everything I was taught before. I
guess I am a Christian-based Religious Scientist."[63] All of
these comments coincide with Rev. E's position that everybody is talking about the same thing ultimately; people just
use different language. I have observed instances of churchgoers who integrate African traditional beliefs, A Course in
Miracles (another spiritual practice that affirms the principle of oneness), and the spiritual aspects of twelve-step
programs into their religious belief systems. Rev. E often
amends the African affirmation, Ahse, to the end of a
prayer, closing with the phrase "Amen, Ahse, And So It Is!"

Moreover, this minister is a prime example of syncretistic religious practice. In addition to welcoming Muslim,
Hindu, and Buddhist speakers to her pulpit on various occasions, she is aware that she has incorporated the Pentecostalism of her youth to her current ministry. She recently
commented:

> I tried not to turn this church into a COGIC church. I tried
> to do the quiet meditative thing, but it just took off. I al-
> ways thought my father's Pentecostal church was too loud
> and boisterous, so when I got this church I didn't want
> that, but because of who I am this is the church I got.
> Wherever you go there you are.[64]

A voice from the congregation responded, "That's OK, we'll
just be the East Bay Church of *Sanctified* Religious Science."

As we have seen, Rev. E does not see any contradiction
in the merging of these two belief systems. She routinely
remarks that Ernest Holmes's philosophy is the same as
what Jesus taught, and she says she learned about spiritual

healing from the old people down South, so she feels that there is no problem in holding the two of them in a healthy tension. I suggest that the religious syncretism of many East Bay churchgoers reveals a comfort level with multiplicity and cultural exchange. Their understanding of religion is not restricted to one set of beliefs as they navigate between multilayered social and religious spaces. An interview respondent noted, "I can live outside the box and accept my divinity and yours." Another said, "A lot of people are not satisfied with the typical Black churches, I like that African Americans at East Bay are free to search for something else."[65] The term "freedom of religion" seems to take on an additional meaning at EBCRS. These church members value their religious practice but don't hold one another to an authenticating set of criteria. They expect that each person will integrate his or her own different experiences and backgrounds into their spiritual practices. This is considered consistent with creating one's own reality, not with blasphemy.

The existence of these combined phenomena at one specific African American church supports the thesis that African American religious expression is more complex than is often suggested by conventional scholarship. The categories classify modes of religious expression at East Bay both in light of their local context and in terms of the contribution these data can make to the general body of African American religious studies. As witness to the intersecting set of phenomena at EBCRS, this study demonstrates that an African American church does not have to remain a bastion of ontological Blackness in order to be considered a legitimate Black church. The EBCRS illustrates that an African American church can thrive by intermingling the more traditional African American cultural aesthetic with the demands of shifting social locations.

5

Methodological Intersections
and Conclusions

Let it be done for you according to your faith.
—Matthew 8:13

Following the terrorist attacks on the United States on September 11, 2001, the Reverend Elouise Oliver admonished the mournful and weeping congregation of the East Bay Church of Religious Science not to divide up humanity into victims and terrorists. She reminded the group that this event could not have happened unless thoughts of hate and violence existed within us all. At the beginning of that service on September 16, 2001, she invited a Muslim to offer the traditional Islamic call to prayer in Arabic. Directed by the scripture Matthew 5:44 to pray for one's enemies, she led a prayer for the terrorists calling for love to conquer hate. Rev. E stated that it was especially important during a time of crisis to remember to look beyond appearances. Quoting Ernest Holmes, she proclaimed, "To desert the Truth in the hour of need is to prove that we did not know the Truth. When things look their worst, that is the supreme moment to demonstrate, to ourselves, that there are no obstructions to the operation of Truth."[1] She instructed the group that while some people held visions of violence and retaliation, she expected this congregation to remain prayerful and hope for love and peace. Following her sermon the choir sang the poignantly relevant Marvin Gaye song "What's Going On" to a standing-room-only crowd of people wailing aloud and holding one another.

This service vividly demonstrates one of the primary teachings of Religious Science: that evil, as a separate entity or being, does not exist. Rather, it is one's consciousness of separation, the falsely held belief that God exists outside of oneself such as in a distant heaven, which limits one's experience of good. Ernest Holmes taught that there is no opposing force to God or goodness. He wrote, "All goodness and every good gift comes from the Father of light. Darkness has no father, but is an illegitimate child of superstition and unbelief, having no parentage in Reality. The Universe is not divided against Itself."[2] The members of East Bay Church of Religious Science refer to "acts and consequences" as a response to the problem of evil.[3] Following Holmes's statement that "we make our own mistakes, suffer our own foolishness," they believe that all things are subject to the principle of cause and effect, or karma, as the Hindu tradition calls it. When an unwanted experience occurs, people of EBCRS are trained to search within themselves to uncover the mental equivalent that brought that experience forth. For it is that diminished state of consciousness that inhibits the good they might otherwise experience. This is held to be true on a social scale as well and accounts for the message Rev. E delivered in the wake of the terrorist attacks of September 11, 2001. Believers understand that their experiences are manifestations of their own mental equivalents.[4] In other words, whatever exists on the outside in the material world cannot exist without there first having been a thought that brought it about and maintains its existence. Nothing that exists on the outside can exist without having a mental equivalent. The manifestation of an enormously tragic event such as this is a reflection of the fear and anger harbored by people on a global scale. Even though a small number of people actually participated, the collective psyche of humankind holds and replicates thoughts of war and destruction as well as xenophobia— fear of those who are different. Religious Science teaches that these things constantly build up and eventually erupt into violence. But, ultimately, the responsibility lies with the consciousness of each individual person, not an embodied, external evil being. Science of Mind, and Rev. E particularly, emphasizes that this religion is about raising the consciousness of every person for the transformation of the entire planet.

Although East Bay Church of Religious Science offers a unique experience of Religious Science, the belief system of the church is well grounded in the teachings of Ernest Holmes. The minister and the congregation closely adhere to his admonition to put the lessons into practice. His often quoted statement on the nature of Religious Science, "Religious Science is a correlation of the Laws of Science, Opinions of Philosophy and revelations of Religion applied to human needs and the aspirations of man," is understood as definitive of the teaching and is printed on the front cover of the church's weekly program. The participants of this church understand the need to be active in changing their own lives, and they believe that EBCRS is a conduit for facilitating such changes. One member of the choir told me, "There ought to be a sign on the door so people know, 'Don't come in here unless you want to be changed.'"[5]

The participants of East Bay Church of Religious Science believe in a monistic, loving, nonpreferential God who has created the universe to operate according to impersonal laws and principles.[6] God is not generally described anthropomorphically, but is sometimes referred to as Father/Mother God. God is believed to be the all-loving, Infinite Intelligence and Universal Mind. The entire created world is an individualized expression of God, and therefore "God is all there is." A common saying at EBCRS is "God operates through me as me." God has experiences through each individual manifestation of itself. Thus, participants of this church believe that there is no separation between God and the individual. All experiences of lack, illness, or unhappiness are grounded in a belief in separation. Spiritual Mind Treatment is prescribed to restore knowledge of the Truth, that there is no separation in God, and anything that appears to be separate is an illusion.

Consistent with the refutation of evil, the people of East Bay Church of Religious Science also reject the Christian idea of original sin and its accompanying need for a savior. During one of her sermons Rev. E proclaimed:

> This is not a church where you have to get saved; you were never lost in the first place. We don't believe that actions can separate people from God. The old-time religion teaches separation and condemnation. They portray God as an angry and vengeful man. Science of Mind teaches that God is Principle, the Thing Itself, to be worshipped in spirit and in truth.[7]

Moreover, the church teaches that the entire universe has been created good, and each human being is God in the flesh. Refuting the idea of a distant God, they claim instead that God is within. In the same sermon Rev. E continued, "We [EBCRS] are about moving closer and closer to our recognition of who we are." Consequently, they affirm their own divinity as individualized expressions of God. Members believe that Jesus' birth story should be understood metaphysically as the story of every person. Jesus is believed to be an exemplar (among others such as Buddha and Gandhi) for his self-knowledge and Christ consciousness. Rev. E frequently refers to Jesus' reported words that whatever he did, others could do to an even greater degree.[8] Interestingly, she lifts up a scripture that is traditionally interpreted as high Christology and reinterprets it as an admonition for every person to become aware of his or her own divine power.

Members of her congregation respond joyfully to this teaching about who they are. They regularly report renewed feelings of confidence and empowerment. People recount their stories during testimonials at Sunday services, during Wednesday night healing services, while sharing with friends in the hallways between services, and in classes. I was consistently told by interview respondents that one of the ways they felt that Religious Science had changed them was in improved confidence. "I broke out of my shyness and began speaking up for myself, because now I know that I am enough. I feel better about myself. This is an empowering teaching."[9] "I have an expanded awareness of my own power."[10] "My understanding of who I am means that I know the power of my word to create any circumstance I want."[11] As accounts like these demonstrate, believers of this philosophy find the teaching of inherent human goodness to be an important part of their religious experience. Since their worldview is one of cocreation, the belief in human value and ability is integral to their existential reality.

These messages of empowerment are couched within the predominant ideology of the church, which rests upon the proposition that the universe is responsive to thoughts, beliefs, and words. Supported by the scripture, "Let it be done for you according to your faith" (Matthew 8:13), the church teaches that individuals are responsible for creating their own circumstances, for better or worse.[12] Whatever exists or "shows up in one's experience" is a result of one's own creation or invitation. This principle is mastered by understanding that thoughts and circumstances are governed by consciousness. The church teaches the importance of raising one's consciousness to the level of "Truth," where there is no separation from the wholeness and perfection of God and all is well. From this perspective the individual believes himself or herself to be strengthened against the influence of appearances upon his or her mind.

For example, when one member was faced with the prospect of homelessness, he put out the word through the community grapevine that he had an immediate need for housing as he only had two weeks before he had to leave his residence. Although he stated the urgency of his situation, he continued to affirm that he would remain steadfast and not be deterred by the appearance of being without a home. He would remain confident and hold the vision that the right situation would show up in time.

Other common situations in which "appearances" are set aside are related to matters of health and finances. The church teaches that illness and lack are not the truth about anyone. Illness and poverty are a result of an impaired consciousness often stemming from deep-seated emotional issues or belief systems that have not been healed or even acknowledged by the individual. Eventually, those feelings and beliefs manifest in the person's physical body and circumstances. Although the church acknowledges that there may be facts that support why a person is ill or poor, such as disease or joblessness, those facts are not the "Truth"— they are appearances and can be changed by using the tools of Religious Science: affirmation, treatment, and meditation. These are offered as how-to methods for getting beyond immediate appearances. Licensed Practitioners may be sought for treatment and counseling when persons are too mired in appearances to see the Truth for themselves. Practitioners are trained to pray and hold a consciousness of Truth for those who cannot do it alone.

Many of my interview participants report that their lives have improved substantially in the areas of health and finance by utilizing these tools. People report that their "income doubled" or that they have "opportunities in areas they never expected" or they experienced improvements in chronic health problems such as diabetes, cancer, and HIV/AIDS.[13] A notable account was offered to me by one person who said he probably would not be alive without the empowerment teachings and practices he gained from Science of Mind, A Course in Miracles, and the twelve-step programs with which he has been involved. He feels that each teaches essentially the same truth, leading to healing through self-empowerment. His personal testimony is heavily influenced by issues of health and recovery. He is recovering from past drug addiction and living with AIDS. In his many years with the disease he has not suffered from opportunistic infections, and only in recent years has he found it necessary to take medications. He credits his health with his belief that in the oneness of God there is no illness, and that within each person there is the power to do all things. He said, "We are all living the one life that is God's life. Through our experiences, God experiences, but it is all one life. Separation is not real. Meditating and doing my affirmations keep me grounded in this truth.[14]

Moreover, this monistic ideology is also manifested in the value system at the church. Two fundamental values among church goers are the recognition of an indwelling divinity in oneself and others, and the practicality of the religion to everyday circumstances. Indwelling divinity is based upon the Science of Mind teaching that each person is an individualized expression of God, who therefore embodies the divine in human form.[15] In turn, this value supports the idea that a life of well-being and abundance is normative. At EBCRS this vision is supported primarily through biblical scripture, the Science of Mind text, and other New Thought literature.[16] When followers are faced with challenges, they are directed to rely upon affirmation, treatment, and meditation to help strip away the facts of the situation in order to get to the Truth. Given the understanding of Truth that all is one and there is no separation, in what untruth is the person participating that has caused the challenge to appear? How might the person be sabotaging his or her own goals? Each person is expected to "go within" or surrender to the indwelling spirit for liberating guidance. Consequently, the church community values the practices of being self reflective and taking ownership of one's own "stuff." Congregants frequently advise one another, "You have to get out of the way of your own stuff and listen to Spirit."

Moreover, the church community values the practical nature of Religious Science. They believe the religion to be a teaching philosophy, putting principle into practice. Ernest Holmes taught that these principles were universal and scientific, meaning they were commonly applicable and replicable in any set of circumstances. To that end, Religious Science churches, including the East Bay Church of Religious Science, emphasize applying these teachings in order to get results in one's life. To the members and regular churchgoers at East Bay, it is second nature to understand spiritual principle and to "work it" to one's advantage.

"Working it" entails using what was referred to earlier as thaumaturgical actions in order to influence one's environment to achieve one's goals and desires. Recall that follow-

ers of thaumaturgical sects take an active role in controlling their environments and experiences through the performance of various types of religious rituals toward the
attainment of the good life (e.g., health, wealth, success).[17]
Likewise, in my interview sessions I asked people if they
regularly made use of Science of Mind teachings in their
daily lives, and I asked if they had experienced any significant changes in their lives that they would attribute to their
participation in Religious Science. The responses were
overwhelmingly affirmative, and I was often able to observe
supporting practices while in the homes of my interview
participants. I found that many people had arranged their
home environments in alignment with particular teachings
for manifesting abundance in the form of health, money,
and relationships. While Religious Science emphasizes the
mental exercise of raising one's consciousness to the level
of divine unity, there are still rituals of sorts that help practitioners to achieve that level of consciousness. These rituals often take the form of making and doing affirmations or
creating a physical space for holding consciousness around
a particular wish.

For example, many people write affirmative statements
and post them on their refrigerators, on bathroom mir-
rors, in hallways, or on closet doors. Some people create
treatment altars where they pray and meditate each day.
One person I visited had a basket of money in her living
room as part of a sacred space that she said reflected the
omnipresent abundance of God. In addition to the basket
overflowing with $1, $5, and $20 bills, she also had symbols
of nature such as leaves, plants, and rocks to further affirm
how the abundance of God manifests itself. She said that
people always comment on the money, but rarely see how
the whole space is integrated to affirm abundance. Her
reason for creating the space, she said, was to see her

abundance.[18] Another person reported that having a morning meditation practice helped to ground him, adding, "I have a lot more peace and humility now." Still another respondent said, "I can control my own destiny, I can take dominion by using these principles and doing my affirmations."[19]

These values and the ideology that supports them are further reinforced in the form of classes and workshops offered as additional tools to help people have positive experiences and achieve their goals. Rev. E strongly encourages people to make use of the courses. In fact, she is so sure that participation in the courses "will change your life" that she offers a money-back guarantee. She says that the majority of her counseling is related to old emotional wounds and negative belief systems that continue to hinder people in their development. Her goal, and the goal of Religious Science, is to teach people that healing is a matter of consciousness, and these tools help people raise their consciousness to the level of health and prosperity.

Workshops are presented by Practitioners or guest ministers. Among the most popular is the weekend-long Inner Child Workshop, facilitated by guest minister David Jones. Some participants find this workshop to be life changing and often repeat it several times as they begin to uncover the original reasons for their beliefs and actions. Also popular is the Soul Processing course taught by visiting minister Brother Ishmael Tetteh of Ghana. He comes to the United States two to four times a year and visits the church to either sit in for Rev. E or teach his soul-processing methods to small groups at EBCRS. Other ongoing workshops cover topics such as forgiveness, healing, and financial abundance. Rev. E sums up the church's ideology in characteristic, self-revelatory terms: "I came in about thirty years ago and it [Religious Science] totally changed my life. I had no car, I was on welfare, but I had the intention to change my life. The intention was the important thing. Life just keeps getting better and better. God wants us all to live in abundance and prosperity. This stuff works, try it and see."[20]

Church services take place in Preservation Park, across the street from the Dellums Federal Building and the California State Building. The park shares the block with the brand new African American Museum and Library and the long-standing First Unitarian Universalist Church. The park is a complex of sixteen restored nineteenth-century Victorian homes, most of which now function as office space. The complex is a beautiful gardenlike environment surrounded by foliage, a wrought iron gate, and a fountain. The space is often used for weddings and photo shoots.

The courtyard atmosphere is conducive to the gathering and mingling of people before and after church services. Each Sunday the courtyard is set up with a hospitality table to welcome visitors and offer general information. Other tables nearby display upcoming events such as concerts, classes, and picnics or sell tapes of previous services and food. Sometimes candid photographs of congregants are on display as well, taken of people as they passed by on their way into service or as they talked with friends outside.

For more than ten years, East Bay Church of Religious Science has held three services in Nile Hall within the Preservation Park complex beginning at 8:00 a.m., 10:00 a.m., and 12:00 p.m. Adjacent to Nile Hall is Ginn House, a space the church uses as a meeting area for after-church activities and as an overflow room where people can see the service on a video monitor if the sanctuary is full. Across the hall from Ginn House is a room set up as the church bookstore. Because Nile Hall was not designed as a church, it takes a lot of effort by many volunteers to turn it into one each Sunday. To accomplish this transformation, chairs are brought in from a storage area and set up; a podium for the minister is brought in, as well as the band instruments, microphones for the choir, an AV system, speakers, a wall clock, flowers, and a wall plaque displaying the denominational "V" symbol; and the bookstore must be set up with books, tables, and a cash register. Simultaneously, the tape ministry is set up in a room connected to the sanctuary to make and duplicate audio cassettes of each service. EBCRS volunteers must clear out of the space immediately following the last service as part of the lease agreement with the complex. While all of this has continued relatively smoothly for years, this type of maintenance has been a critical reason for enabling the church to keep its own space. As I neared the end of my fieldwork, EBCRS was in the process of moving into a new church home, having secured a new property at 4130 Telegraph Avenue.

I have attended most of the Sunday services at the East Bay Church of Religious Science for the past six years. However, since I began the work of purposefully observing and collecting information two years ago, I brought my ethnographer's eye to this eventful worship service. This means that I took on the role of observing, experiencing, and participating in conversations and other daily activities with the community members and recording these observations.[21]

On any given Sunday, the formal order of service is essentially the same. Services begin promptly on the hour with meditation. Those who wish to participate must be on time, because once the meditation begins, the doors are closed and no one may enter until it is over. Meditation is led by the Practitioner whose duty it is to act as pulpit assistant for that Sunday. While soft music plays, the Practitioner attempts to focus the meditation around a general theme and at selected intervals interjects a word or a phrase to help anchor everyone to the theme. At the conclusion of the meditation, the doors to the sanctuary are opened to allow the rest of the congregants to enter. By this time, people have gathered at all of the sanctuary doors, waiting for the opportunity to get in and find their favorite seat. While this creates a stir within the room, the Practitioner continues reading the weekly announcements, after which time the choir processes into the sanctuary from a side entrance. The mass choir enters exuberantly with the processional song. Their entry immediately engages everyone in the room.

Dressed in color coordinated ensembles, singing boldly and clapping their hands, the choir is led in by the musical director in time to an African worship song, getting the congregation on its feet, clapping and singing along to the familiar tune. Once the choir has taken its position on the raised dais of the sanctuary behind the minister's pulpit, it begins to sing one of the selections for the day. Most of the time the congregation joins in with singing, dancing, waving of hands, and playing of tambourines. On many occasions, individual members have spontaneously jumped from their seats and danced their way to the front of the sanctuary, where they continued dancing for the duration of the song. During the quieter songs, members of the congregation participate by standing and slowly swaying or rocking side to side in their seats. The ushers walk around with boxes of tissue, offering them to tearful worshipers. After the first song, the Practitioner leads the congregation in prayer and in reciting the "Declaration of Principles." The congregants are asked to stand for the reading of the Principles, as the Practitioner recites them and the people repeat them. The choir then sings a second song, after which the minister, Rev. E, comes to the pulpit.

She is customarily dressed in regal style, wearing an African-inspired, colorful long dress, and head wrap. If she feels particularly moved by the choir or if she feels the group needs more music ministry, she directs the choir to "keep on singin'." After the choir has finished, she begins her message by leading the group in singing the congregational song, "I Woke Up This Morning," an uptempo, hand-clapping song. At the conclusion of this song, congregants remain standing to recite the congregational statement. Just as the Practitioner led the "Declaration of Principles" by call and response, Rev. E leads the statement in the same manner as follows:

> God is the only Power in my life.
> Nothing from without can touch the perfect life of God within me. No past experience has power over me.
> I am a perfect child of God and nothing that any one has ever done or said can interfere with my divine inheritance.
> The Power of God is Greater than any circumstance in my life. The strength of God is mine to use. Turning away from all feeling of inadequacy, I discover that all that I need is within me right now.
> As I forgive the past, I find that I have nothing to atone for and nothing run away from.
> Casting off the old me, I discover my true self.
> I take dominion in my life. Old habits have no power over me. Conditions have no power, personalities have no power. I take dominion.
> I am whole I am complete and I am free. Now and forever more
> And so it is, YES!

The congregation is then seated and the sermon begins. Sermon topics are listed in the church programs and usually emphasize the practical nature of Science of Mind teachings. Rev. E shares experiences from her own life. She uses the Science of Mind textbook and the Bible to support her teaching. In order to highlight the real-life applicability of the philosophy, she encourages individuals to give testimony of their own experiences. When testimonials are given, they normally fit into the order of service just before Rev. E comes to the pulpit.

While giving testimony is a common feature in a traditional African American Christian church, it is a rather recent phenomenon at East Bay Church of Religious Science Sunday services, although the Wednesday evening services have routinely provided a space for this. Rev. E refers to this practice as something from the "old church" that helps the rest of the congregation see that God (Universal Spirit) works for everyone. She often references the scripture that God is no respecter of persons; what God does for one, God will do for all. In the "old church," testimony may be couched in the folk vernacular as examples of "how I got over" or "what the Lord has done for me" as a specific intention to reflect one's faith in Jesus or to show the unmerited grace of God. Often, testimonials come out of experiences of students who are in the process of taking the first-level Foundations class. Rev. E takes the opportunity to share the transformations that emerge in class with the whole congregation.

Although there is no Religious Science lectionary to follow, churches who are members of the United Church of Religious Science (UCRS) are encouraged by the home office each January to organize their sermons around the basic teachings of Science of Mind as they are laid out in the first four chapters of the textbook. East Bay Church of

Religious Science follows this guideline, and so begins by teaching the following lessons over the first four weeks of January: The Thing Itself, The Way It Works, What It Does, and How to Use It. In this way, churchgoers are reminded of the foundational material each new year.

Rev. E concludes each sermon by receiving the "treatment box" from a Practitioner or Practitioner student, in which anyone may place a request, and she offers an affirmative prayer/treatment for these requests and the general congregational body. This is followed by an acknowledgment of visitors, who are asked to stand and are given large pink envelopes containing information about the church and the denomination while the congregation warmly welcomes them with applause. Rev. E invites the visitors to return and offers to meet them after service to shake hands and partake in fellowship.

At this time, Practitioners are asked to stand and be recognized as "Prayer Warriors who love to pray" and are available at any time to pray with people individually. Thought they are generally distinguishable by their purple stoles, they may not be wearing them on any given Sunday, thus they are specifically pointed out in service. They also have designated seats throughout the sanctuary identified by purple hoods fitted over the backs of chairs. Prayer sessions can be arranged immediately following the service, or members may call a Practitioner during the week.

Next is the reading of the offering statement and collection of tithes and offerings. Ushers come forward and gather small baskets while the following statement is recited by all:

As I tithe I demonstrate abundance to the Glory of God Who lives and expresses as me. I dare to give freely, knowing that I cannot outgive God. For God's business is my business and God's business is good. And so it is!

Following the statement, the musicians play softly and the ushers pass around the baskets to receive the offerings. The collection is gathered into one large basket and taken from the sanctuary. Then the congregation stands and recites "The Prayer of Faith," followed by a closing song such as "The Unity Song"; the minister concludes with the benediction. The congregation is dismissed and people file out, hugging and mingling with one another. Friends spot one another across the room and rush to greet each other. Some visit the bookstore or line up outside to purchase audio tapes of the sermon. Parents retrieve their small children from Junior Church, and the older youth, who have been in Teen Church, hang around waiting to find their parents leaving the sanctuary.

While this is the general order of the service, there are atypical services as well that recognize particular events such as a guest speaker, a Practitioner installment service, or a baptism. Baptisms present an interesting opportunity to observe the union of a traditional Christian ritual through the lens of Religious Science. I have observed a number of baptisms during the years of my attendance at the church and during my period of field research. Typically, baptisms are offered on fifth Sundays, so ceremonies are only conducted in certain months that accommodate five Sundays.

One baptism I observed was the first to take place in the new facility. It was fit into the order of service following the choir's second song. Rev. E invited parents, godparents, and children to the front of the sanctuary. The parents took turns introducing their children and extended family members, and then Rev. E. proceeded with the baptism of each child. This day there were seven children, all of whom appeared to be under the age of two years, though some were clearly infants. The ceremony began with Rev. E's speech about the meaning of baptism. She said, "Baptism is an outward manifestation of the inward spiritual transformation." Referencing the scripture Luke 18:15, she continued that baptism of children is a recognition of the loving presence and Spirit in a child. She admonished parents and godparents to set an example for the children by living their lives by divine principle and thus teaching the child these principles.

Rev. E then proceeded with the baptismal rite itself. Dressed in all white with her hair tied up in an African-style head wrap, she asked the congregation to welcome the children into the community of the East Bay Church of Religious Science. While the piano played softly, she began to address each child:

> [Child's name] I christen you in the name of the Father, Son and Holy Spirit. The Father is the principle in whom you live, the Son is the Christ consciousness within you and the Holy Spirit is the moving creative principle of all life. Oh, Infinite Intelligence I dedicate this child to thy care and keeping . . . and thy unfailing wisdom will guide and direct this child and [that] your love will draw her into happiness and eternal life.

Then she sprinkled the child with water from a yellow rose dipped into a small glass bowl of water held by a pulpit assistant. As she completed the rite with one child, she proceeded one by one down the line until all the children had been baptized. She then released the families, to be seated again among the congregation. The service then continued in customary order as described above.

Some of the other recurring rituals at EBCRS include "Perfect Partner Sunday," the Forty Day Prosperity Program, and New Practitioner Induction Ceremonies. Perfect Partner Sunday is an annual ceremony fit into the order of service that encourages the single people in the congregation to affirm the presence of a perfect partner into their lives. This ritual involves asking the single people to stand and recite an affirmation that both addresses the individual's state of mind around relationship issues and calls for the right relationship to manifest for them. On some of these occasions, the participants were encouraged to pin flowers to their clothes, so that everyone could see who was single and seeking a partner.

The Forty Day Prosperity program is an exercise in manifesting financial abundance. This ritual involves committing oneself to forty days of purposeful reading, meditation, and journaling on the principles outlined in a Science of Mind booklet called *The Abundance Book,* by John Randolph Price. This booklet contains ten affirmations to help the reader focus on the oneness of all things and to remember that the ultimate source of all things is God. The reader is taught to rely on this ultimate source and not to look to one's circumstances for sustenance. The practitioner is required to read and meditate on one of the ten affirmations per day, repeating the cycle four times for a total of forty days. Journaling is also an important part of the process in order to help expand the individual's awareness around issues of prosperity. This process requires forty consecutive days. If a day is missed, the individual must start over at day one. It is taught that a shift in consciousness requires consistent, focused effort. Sometimes Rev. E leads the church through a forty-day cycle, checking in each Sunday to see that people are still on course. Mostly, however, individuals decide to do so for themselves, or they form small groups to support one another through the full program. The cycle may be repeated consecutively or as one feels the need in one's own life.

The New Practitioner Induction Ceremony commemorates four years of course work and licensing by the United Church of Religious Science organization. The induction is performed as a very solemn, sacred event at EBCRS. As lay leaders, the Practitioners are highly valued and recognized within the church, and welcoming new people into the group is a significant event in the life of the church.

I attended a noontime induction ceremony that took place as part of the third service in Nile Hall, which is indicative of this annual event. The sanctuary was filled to capacity with church members, regular attendees, visitors, and family members of the new Practitioners. People stood along the walls throughout the room, in some places standing two deep from the wall. The lighting in the room was dimmed, and the Practitioner inductees walked in, followed by the current corps of Practitioners. As they slowly proceeded down the center aisle of the church, the band played a rendition of a Michael Jackson song, "Will You Be There." All were dressed in ivory clothing, some in dresses, some in long tunic and pant ensembles, some in formal evening suits, and each held an electric candle that illuminated the darkened room.

The installment was facilitated by the president of the Practitioner corps. She led the group in the taking of their vows, initiating a call and response ritual in which the group response to each of her admonitions was, "Yes, I am a healing presence." At the conclusion of the recitations, the president came forth to place the traditional purple stole around the neck of each new Practitioner, symbolically acknowledging their new status. The choir director quietly sang "Standing on the Promise" as all the Practitioners took their seats in a specially designated area of the church that occupied half of the right side of the room.

At this time the children and young adults were led out to junior and teen church, respectively, while the lights in the sanctuary were raised and the church service proceeded as usual with the singing of the congregational song, followed by the call and response Declaration of Principles.

The new designation of licensed Practitioner indicates a commitment of the person to the service of the church and its community. In addition, each person is licensed to charge fees for his or her services, and they may use the designation "RScP" following their names, meaning Religious Science Practitioner. This level of licensing is mandatory for those who intend to progress further into ministerial school or to advanced levels of leadership, such as administrator at the Los Angeles home office.

Assessment of Interviews

I began this work with the hypothesis that the main reason the East Bay Church of Religious Science is successful with a predominantly African American congregation is due to the intersection of an empowering New Thought teaching and an embodied presence of an African American cultural aesthetic found in the community there. Thus, I designed my questions to be open-ended in order to allow the participants to explain in their own words what keeps them coming back to the church. From their comments I have been able to elicit at least some of the key factors in the EBCRS church experience.

One event that happened early on in my research confirmed that I was on the right track. During a break at one of the evening Foundational classes that I attended, a woman, whom I had just met and with whom I was making small talk about something Rev. E had said in class, announced, "You know Rev. E is straight up Pentecostal. You wouldn't get this at any other Religious Science church."[22] Since this was not in an interview context, just a conversational moment I was both surprised and encouraged by her extemporaneous comment about Rev. E's influences and how they show up within the church.

I have come to learn more about the meaning of "you wouldn't get *this* at any other Religious Science church." My interviews have made it clear that East Bay Church of Religious Science stands out from other Religious Science churches in terms of its liturgical style and general "feel." Many people have made comments similar to Rev. E's own statement that she did not feel like she had "had church" when she first started attending the Unity church with her mother-in-law because the church was so quiet. Likewise, a few of my conversation partners shared that during visits to other Religious Science churches they have been surprised by the hushed services. One person remarked that when he attended First Church of Religious Science (a mostly White congregation in Oakland), he greatly missed the energy of the Black church. He noted that the people were friendly, but that there was rarely any music, and that the congregation had a very composed atmosphere. He said he did not feel completely satisfied in that environment.[23]

In another conversation a woman told me that she travels throughout California regularly and has visited other Religious Science churches in Stockton, Lodi, Vallejo, Los Angeles, Monterey, and even in Maui, Hawaii. She found that EBCRS stands apart from all of them for its energy. She reported that these churches use more of a lecture style without scriptural references rather than the sermon style used by Rev. E, and that the music is folksy or new age, not gospel. She said that East Bay Church has a "spirit-filled joy," while the people at the other churches seemed happy but reserved. Finally, she commented that these other churches had much smaller congregations, ranging from twenty to fifty people, a large contrast to the thousand-plus membership of EBCRS.[24]

There is a large overlap in interview responses that describe EBCRS as "not a typical Black church" but that it retains the cultural elements of African Americans and the worship style commonly found in African American churches, particularly from the Pentecostal Church of God in Christ denomination. In response to my question, "Does the racial makeup of the church impact the nature or style of the services?" one respondent remarked, "Yes, there's a vibe, not [like] a typical Black church, but it has those ingredients."[25] When asked to clarify the meaning of "those ingredients," this respondent answered, "You know, Black flavor." Another person responded with "there's got to be some Afrocentricity, White churches are boring, they have no flavor. At least a diverse mix makes it more interesting."[26]

After hearing "Black flavor" mentioned by four different people in separate circumstances, I decided to ask interview participants about their notions of Blackness in terms of religion and worship styles. I asked if there are specific elements that stand out in their mind as being characteristic of an African American church. Descriptions ranged from "lots of whoopin' and hollerin'," gospel music, soulfulness, and emotionalism, to charismatic ministers, formal dress, and long services. In addition, eleven different people described Black churches as "openly expressive of spirit."[27] These same people went on to give independent descriptions of Black people as being "religiously open, soulful, expressive, and rhythmic." I was told that these feelings are "obviously carried over from who Black people are wherever they go," and, therefore, that East Bay Church simply reflects the cultural expressions of the dominant population group.[28]

The fact that these cultural elements are flourishing at East Bay Church of Religious Science is usually attributed to Rev. E herself. In addition to the idea that the church reflects the dominant cultural group of the congregants, members acknowledge that Rev. E is at the heart of the worship style. In a conversation, one member told me, "On some level all of us can relate to her."[29] Another person reported, "Rev. E speaks her messages from her experiences as a southern Black woman, but all people can feel comfortable here."[30] An additional respondent added, "We wouldn't have half of the soul [that we have] if it wasn't for having an African American at the helm. It's one of the most wonderful things. Even though [Religious Science] was started by a White person EBCRS is basically a Black church."[31]

This last statement is quite significant in that it seems to represent the congregants' general feeling about the church. They clearly feel that they have adapted the religion to fit their needs, regardless of the founder's race. Yet, there are challenges. Rev. E recalls a debate that arose around a statement from an earlier edition of the Science of Mind textbook. As she tells it, in Ernest Holmes's attempt to describe the universal applicability of Science of Mind principles, he wrote that "even the most misshapen beings in darkest Africa could use these teachings and benefit from them." Although she is unclear about the year, she remembers that it was East Bay Church's minister of education at the time, the Reverend FranCion, who pressed the United

Church of Religious Science for removal of the statement. It was eventually edited out. Rev. FranCion later served as the director of education for the Holmes Institute in Los Angeles, the ministerial training branch of the United Church of Religious Science. Rev. E attributes this sort of insensitivity to the general racism that exists throughout American institutions. She does not believe that it is present more within Religious Science than anywhere else in society. She states, "You can find racism anywhere. A lot of times people are not even aware that something is offensive until it is pointed out. So that is what you have to do sometimes." She was not discouraged by incidents like these because she believes in the power of Science of Mind principles and wants African Americans to receive them. She says, "Black people are the ones who need to know about them [the principles] most."

While it is clear that the members and regular worshipers at East Bay Church of Religious Science enjoy the African American cultural elements they find there, the point must also be made that nearly all of my respondents value the message they receive as much as the cultural familiarity they experience. "I like the fellowship, the integrity of people, the message of health, peace, abundance, and how I can really apply it to my life."[32] Another respondent added, "The minister's messages are phenomenal, they hit me right in my heart, it works for me."[33]

In some cases, respondents seem to privilege having access to what they believe to be spiritual truth and the message of empowerment over the importance of an African American majority culture. Even those who say that an African American culture is only somewhat important to them personally also feel it as a pleasant bonus to have Religious Science teaching within a culturally African American congregation. As one respondent said, "It's not necessary to be at an African American church at this point in my life. I'm more concerned about hearing truth that resonates with me, but I love Black people, so I go to East Bay."[34] One Practitioner said, "It [East Bay] is a part of me and what I do. It is supportive, joyful, rejuvenating. I finally found a marriage of philosophy and Black experience. I had always had to sacrifice one or the other."[35] Others acknowledged explicitly that they feel more comfortable at a predominantly African American church, and therefore appreciate East Bay Church that much more. "East Bay speaks to my soul. That's why I go to a Black church. I can be myself, and I can exhale."[36] Another noted:

> It's important for me to have the Black Experience and I get it there. Black people share common life experiences, it's like knowing the taste of banana pudding, you can know about it, but it's different to have tasted it yourself. We have shared experiences and that makes a difference.[37]

It is evident that these members and church participants value East Bay Church for the interconnection of a spiritual teaching that empowers them and for an African American cultural aesthetic that supports them. From their own comments it is apparent that the church successfully serves their needs both religiously and culturally. Success for this church is also marked by the fact that people claim that it supports their use of Science of Mind principles and that these principles work for them in their daily lives. Another measure of success is the positive word-of-mouth reputation that the church has enjoyed, swelling the membership rolls from thirty-seven people in the mid-1970s to more than one thousand during Rev. E's tenure as minister.[38]

Models of African American Aesthetics

An important part of this project has been looking at how an African American aesthetic has impacted Religious Science. To define this aesthetic is a complex undertaking even as I limit my field to African American cultural and worship styles. These complexities are inherent in any conversation or effort to define race, and more specifically Blackness. For instance, in what terms does one begin to define authentic Blackness, biology, culture, socialization, performance, attitude, politics, religion, class, or some combination of them? Does the embodiment of one or more of these things affirm authenticity, or the lack thereof reveal inauthenticity? What is authenticity? Do you just know it when you see it? One scholar defines it as "being able to negotiate specific behaviors and cultural codes that will allow for 'proper' categorization."[39] As scholarly works show, all of these elements must be grappled with to some extent. Moreover, I suggest that there is an intensity to racial discourses that reflects the American preoccupation with racial identification and categorization.

At least partially in response to White supremacist ideologies that dehumanized Blacks on the basis of race, African Americans have made significant efforts to establish their own markers of identity. The efforts of historical figures such as W. E. B. Du Bois, Booker T. Washington, Marcus Garvey, Martin Luther King, Jr., and others to defend Black humanity and to seek their uplift were therefore usually carried out by appealing to a set of race-based apologetics. Contemporary scholars must acknowledge the circumstances under which those older standards were established while building new ones that recognize the multiple social locations that Black people occupy. To illustrate how multilayered this exercise of identifying an African American aesthetic can be, I review some of the efforts from noted scholars on the so-called traditional view and the so-called new Black aesthetic.

The traditional view has supported an African American cultural aesthetic around the following shared memory experiences: an African worldview that asserts the divinity of all aspects of the creation, the Middle Passage, the American slave trade, southern rural life, the ensuing struggles for freedom and justice that gave birth to the civil rights movement, and the ongoing collective experiences of Black people in the United States.[40] Scholars who have written from this perspective include C. Eric Lincoln and Lawrence H. Mamiya and James H. Evans. Lincoln and Mamiya refer to this set of circumstances as constitutive of "Black consciousness," which they define as an existential shift among Black people that yielded new perceptions of self and society, and growth in self-confidence and self-respect.[41] Black consciousness signified a movement from humble agricultural life toward a recognition of selfhood and new possibilities. Evans incorporates the traditional model of Black experience theologically when he writes:

> African-American theological development can be best understood as the convergence of an African derived worldview, the complexities of the experiences of slavery, oppression, survival, rebellion, and adjustment in the New World, and their encounter with the biblical text. These realities shaped the African-American intellect and spirit.[42]

Likewise, many scholars of Black theology also regard these experiences as paradigmatic of the Black experience. The list of scholars includes but is not limited to Dwight Hopkins, Will Coleman, Katie Cannon, and Delores Williams, who have fought for the legitimacy of creating liberating theologies using resource material from the context of African American experiences. In an attempt to privilege non-European theological sources, these scholars and others have turned to slave narratives, biographical material, Negro spirituals, and African traditional religious material as means of validating Black encounters with God. These resources are appropriated in an effort to recapture authenticity, to help Black people reconnect with material that addresses their own experiences. They suggest a reliance upon the traditional aesthetic in the sense that they reflect Black lives characterized by poverty, the struggle against oppression, southern rural culture, and appropriations of African epistemologies.

Even as these scholars' works support the traditional Black aesthetic, the standard is challenged to respond to shifts in the social climate. For example, in the era following the Second World War, the southern folk model of authentic Blackness naturally underwent some revision as many African Americans began the exodus out of southern rural areas into urban metropolises. Whereas the northern migration did not eliminate issues of racism, segregation, poverty, and oppression, African Americans arrived with hopes for more opportunities and substantially better lifestyles than the South had offered them. The stress of transitioning from the agricultural to the industrial was often exacerbated by the circumstances of living in ghettoized cities and competing with immigrant communities such as the Irish for jobs. History reveals that when these opportunities did not materialize as expected, political activism was recognized as an important component of African American identity.

The contemporary social climate is now a technology-based global economy that calls for people who are

comfortable with simultaneous existence in multiple categories. Whereas the intention of traditional models of authenticity was for uplift and empowerment, the categorical
standard that arose in that context cannot be used to ostra-
cize other African American people who would choose to
occupy these multiple spaces. Hence, the social climate
now calls for a new African American aesthetic that can
embrace difference without sacrificing legitimacy.

> The advocates of a revised African-American aesthetic as-
> sert that a cultural politics of difference is more adequate
> for the dynamic, contemporary experiences of African-
> Americans.[43] Such a system acknowledges the "axes of diff-
> erence experienced by each Black or American who is some
> specific gender, sexual orientation, class or social standing,"
> all of which have become more intertwined since the latter
> part of the 20th century.[44] Scholars such as Victor Ander-
> son, bell hooks and J. Martin Favor agree that traditional or
> classic categories of Black identity based around enslave-
> ment, poverty and oppression lead to a definition where
> Blackness is equated with suffering.[45] Rather than perpetu-
> ate a set of characterizations where *authentic* Blackness is
> couched in terms of pathology and crisis, there is a growing
> body of scholars who implore a movement in the discourse
> that allows African-Americans to transcend these circum-
> stances and pursue their own paths of fulfillment without
> risk of ostracization from the group.[46]

J. Martin Favor's work serves as an example to the discussion of transgressing racial categorization. In his book
Authentic Blackness: The Folk in the New Negro Renaissance,
Favor looks at how issues of class, gender, and geography
were applied as markers of racial authenticity among the
literary works of the Harlem Renaissance era. He posits

that the normative value assigned to the southern, rural, poor Black folk in literary criticism reflected the actual normativity assigned to Black folk in defining Black identity at that time.[47] To help him explore why these folk experiences were foregrounded when there were obviously other types of Black experiences, Favor focuses on the literature offered by some Black authors of the 1920s to 1930s that challenged adherence to a folk-based model of authenticity.[48] He notes that when racial authenticity is tied too closely to class, gender, and geography, the middle class or at least the nonfolk are excluded from what is fundamentally or distinctly African American.[49] Likewise, Victor Anderson, whose work suggests a revision of the classic Black aesthetic, expands Favor's comment to include that any objective marker of racial authenticity will result in insiders and outsiders within the group.

Similarly, Anderson and hooks argue against the classical Black aesthetic, stating that it is too narrow and excludes too many African Americans whose life choices may fall outside of the traditional prescription. Anderson says that the classical aesthetic has produced an "ontological Blackness," a phrase he uses as "a covering term connoting categorical, essentialist, and representational languages depicting black life and experience."[50] He further writes, "I share with [bell] hooks a deep suspicion about the ways that this racial aesthetic conceals levels of cultural differentiation among African-Americans."[51] Anderson here refers to hooks's position that the classical Black aesthetic has often subordinated Black women's issues. She questions the idea that in the struggle for Black liberation, race has always trumped gender, sexuality, and class issues. Both agree on the need to press beyond the classical Black aesthetic on the simple basis that such a model is ineffectual for describing the conditions of postmodern North American life. hooks contrasts the classic aesthetic by suggesting a "Postmodern Blackness," an idea that accommodates the widely differentiated social spaces and communities that African Americans inhabit.[52] She recognizes that African Americans are continuously negotiating these multiple locations and therefore advocates for a new identity language that better describes their experiences under changing social conditions.[53]

When all is said and done, an insistence upon racial definition presumes that there exists an ideal set of criteria that, when identified, can be an accurate and effective tool. However, this presumption only raises more questions about authenticity and opens the way for other forms of racial stereotyping. As each of these scholars has pointed out, Black people simultaneously occupy more than one social location. If this basic issue is not considered, then racial stereotyping still provides the standard for representation. Reification of racial stereotypes can occur based on narrowly defined standards of authentic Blackness established by African American intellectuals who seek to combat the dehumanizing claims of White racists, just as they have occurred based on the categorical racism of White supremacist ideologies.

As one attempt to avoid a new set of race-based stereotypes, Favor supports the idea of the "cultural mulatto," a term he found among the works of writer Trey Ellis that describes a member of the New Black Aesthetic as one who

> has been educated by a multi-racial mix of cultures, [and] can also navigate easily in the White world. Additionally, as cultural mulattoes we no longer need to deny or suppress any part of our complicated and sometimes contradictory cultural baggage to please either White or Black people.[54]

While this description has its own limitations and invites a critique of membership in the New Black Aesthetic, Ellis seems to be offering a definition or way of speaking about Blackness that acknowledges the dynamics of multiplicity without sacrificing racial authenticity. His attempt at a definition shows up the inherent in-group and out-group problem associated with categorization. The complexities cannot be resolved here. I defer to the question Favor asks at the end of his work, "Do we really need a 'grand unifying theory' of Black identity when comparing and contrasting a plurality of positions is immensely instructive in its own right?"[55]

The East Bay Church of Religious Science is a point of instruction. This church stands as a noteworthy intersection between the two major schools of thought on what comprises a Black cultural aesthetic. On one hand, the church's worship services exhibit the classic Black cultural aesthetic informed by a set of collective memories peculiar to Black people in North America. These shared memories consist of retained African cultural remnants, the collective experiences of slavery and rural life, as well as the struggles for freedom, equality, and empowerment.

Moreover, this aesthetic contributes to a certain performed aspect of culture that often manifests itself in African American religious expressions. Lincoln and Mamiya connect the performed aspects of rhythmic music and dance with an embodied African worldview or Black sacred cosmos that "surges and erupts" in African American religious expression in a qualitatively different cultural form than is found in White religious expression.[56] Following upon the insights of Du Bois, who wrote in *Souls of Black Folk* that the key religious elements he found in Black churches was "the preacher, the music and the frenzy,"[57] Lincoln and Mamiya add, "Du Bois was referring to the intense enthusiasm and the open display of emotion and feelings exhibited by the worshippers."[58] Thus, from collective memories and shared experiences the cultural aesthetic is formed, which in turn shapes an African American aesthetic.

On the other hand, EBCRS also manifests a new aesthetic characterized by a "cultural politics of difference," in that it is church home to people of different classes, sexualities, and economic levels, none of which are considered to compromise the authenticity of Blackness. This model is espoused by revisionists like Anderson, hooks, and Favor. Not only is the church a locus for Black people of varying backgrounds, it also represents a fluid mode of African American religiosity. The theological and philosophical systems at EBCRS transgress traditional models of African American religious practices. "Authentic" African American religion has been centered upon a liberating form of Christianity that ministers to a struggling, oppressed people.[59] This model offered African Americans personal redemption and a foundation for uplift from social oppression. However, followers of this Christian model were also encouraged toward complacency and to internalize what Anthony Pinn calls the "theodical game" of redemptive suffering in which oppression is accorded some positive value that would ultimately be rewarded in the next life.[60] Not surprisingly, these concepts have been problematic for attaining the freedom and equality that African Americans initially connected with Christianity.[61]

At East Bay Church of Religious Science, the concepts of struggle, oppression, redemptive suffering, and financial lack have been reinterpreted. Although the church has a predominantly African American membership, it does not affirm concepts that have traditionally meant authenticity for African American religion. Religious Science teachings affirm that individual freedom, divine connectedness, health, wealth, and well-being represent the natural, legitimate conditions for all humans, race notwithstanding. Under the older model, these instances of "difference" immediately marginalize Religious Science as a religious practice for African Americans and renders East Bay Church of Religious Science inauthentic as a "Black church." This example highlights the problem associated with remaining strictly within the realm of the traditional or classic Black aesthetic. A revision of that aesthetic is required, one that does not belittle the cohesive value of the historical memories that African Americans share, but also does not prevent Blacks from whole participation within the ever-changing contexts of life in the twenty-first century. The East Bay Church of Religious Science is an example of what a community can look like when individual Black people are not forced to choose between their racial authenticity and other (religious, sexual, socioeconomic) aspects of themselves.

East Bay Church represents a phenomenon of intersecting traits of African American shared historical memories, performed culture, and a cultural politics of difference. I contend that these particular aspects of the African American cultural aesthetic infuse the Science of Mind philosophy at East Bay Church of Religious Science, creating a unique worship experience.

6

Implications for the Future

"Coming to a Church Near You"

One of the goals of this book has been to acknowledge and illuminate the multiplicities of African American religious expressions. In doing so, I have presented the experiences of a particular Religious Science community to demonstrate how its members are helped by what they have found there. This final chapter will discuss some of the social and scholarly implications of the growth of African American membership in these types of churches. In addition, I present some of the developments which seem to be on the horizon for New Thought, and I take a final look at the East Bay Church of Religious Science.

The proliferation of New Thought churches among African Americans indicates that many of their needs are being met through these religious systems. What these needs are has shifted over time. As we have seen historically, the first focus for African Americans who were carving out a place for themselves in the United States was to meet their needs for basic freedom and justice. Through grassroots efforts and civil rights activities, these needs began to stabilize; but other needs, such as economic opportunity and life satisfaction, began to take prominence. In the contemporary sociocultural context in which the

next level of the civil rights movement has been acknowledged by many community leaders as economic empowerment for African Americans, it is not surprising that this
challenge is reflected in religious expressions because historically African Americans have used religious avenues as
a means of achieving social goals.[1] Therefore, it is not surprising that some of the African American churches that
are experiencing substantial growth espouse prosperity
and personal empowerment.

As Joseph Washington wrote in 1964, Black religion has
to serve the needs of Black people or else it ceases to help
them attain freedom, and thus ceases to be the religion of
the folk. Without renewing the controversy surrounding
Washington's assessment of the efficacy of institutional
Black churches versus folk religion, I use his understanding
of folk religion to describe a type of religion that meets the
needs of the people it serves. Following Washington in this
respect, I affirm that freedom also encompasses economic
prosperity, and, therefore, a relevant Black religion in the
current context would need at least to address matters of
economic empowerment, if not actively provide believers
with sets of tools to help them achieve it. Whether couched
in the language of Christianity or New Thought, prosperity
teachings are receiving more respectability now than when
people like Rev. Ike and Daddy Grace were first preaching
from storefront churches. The success that New Thought
teachings are finding among African Americans offers new
insight into the ways that different religions are providing
empowerment for their followers.

As we have seen, New Thought provides tools for individual empowerment. This differs significantly from the
communal emphasis of the traditional Black religions. The
teachings are centered on personal uplift, personal empowerment, and personal achievement through the raising of

individual consciousness. The philosophy does not overtly seek to answer questions of worldwide suffering or poverty. Individual concerns appear to be elevated over the concerns of the community. For African Americans, this would seem to be a divergence from historical cultural norms that still reflect an African worldview which seeks the welfare of the community over the individual.[2]

Religiously, this community commitment has been apparent in the many church-based struggles for freedom and justice throughout African American history. Thus, an important question to consider for an African American follower of New Thought is, to what extent does this philosophy contribute to the "uplift of the race"? Followed by: to what extent is this important to them? Traditionally, African Americans have considered this command to be a critical component of their religious practices since the experiences of slavery. Freedom and uplift have been considered the crux of Black religion.[3] Perhaps the presence of African Americans in New Thought suggests a belief that the uplift of the race can occur one individual at a time. This would be a relatively new phenomenon for Black religious expressions. It is a view that I suspect might be problematic for those who have more traditional religious expectations, leading back to the complex discussion of trying to define authentic Blackness by one's political and religious beliefs. Though I have argued that an African American presence in New Thought presses beyond categories of ontological Blackness, when we acknowledge how black religions have functioned historically these categories once again come to the surface. For African Americans, race and religion have been historically intermingled. How might New Thought religions address such matters of communal significance for African Americans? Is it possible for this religious philosophy to provide a directive for community progress, or does it remain primarily a religion for individual enlightenment?

Recent activities among some New Thought churches suggest a desire to address communal and global issues. Toward the end of my research at East Bay Church of Religious Science, I began to note that some New Thought groups were becoming galvanized in that direction. Through an encounter with one of the ministers of the well-known Agape International Spiritual Center in Los Angeles, I discovered that there is a burgeoning movement among several New Thought organizations, including the United Church of Religious Science, Religious Science International, and the Association for Global New Thought to contribute to the relief of poverty and violence around the world. Specifically, the United Church of Religious Science is active in South Africa, addressing some of the current social issues such as HIV/AIDS, crime, racism, and lack of education. For UCRS, this work is part of a mission called the Global Heart Vision, a three-year-old outreach program designed to address issues of homelessness, violence, war, hunger, separation, and disenfranchisement. Local churches and communities are charged to become "points of inspiration and influence effectively advancing the vision of Global Heart through its ministries and transformative teaching." Agape is one church that has been ahead of this movement. In 1994 this community established an international outreach ministry called Globalworks, which has been attending to the spiritual and material needs of people in Brazil, Nigeria, Argentina, Russia, Bahamas, Jamaica, and South Africa. While I am not aware of any such programs coming from the EBCRS specifically, I now realize that considerations for the worldwide community are being made by various New Thought organizations. Perhaps missionary work represents the next phase of growth for New Thought.

Another area of discontinuity between New Thought religions and mainstream Christian Black churches is in the matter of female leadership. A look at any roster of New Thought churches reveals a preponderance of female pastors, which is a significant change from the traditional viewpoint still held by many Christians that women should not occupy this role. Among African American Christians, this view is maintained by many Missionary Baptists, Pentecostals, and of course Catholics. Rev. E has said this stance was one of the main reasons she left the Pentecostal denomination, not believing that such a teaching could be God's truth. Her beliefs were affirmed when she discovered female pastors in the Unity church, and thus Unity and later Religious Science represented new faiths in which she could be fully accepted.

It is likely that the strong presence of female pastors in New Thought churches is the result of a rich legacy of women's leadership throughout the history of the movement. As we have seen, many New Thought institutions were founded or led by women, including Mary Baker Eddy, Emma Curtis Hopkins, Myrtle Fillmore, Malinda Cramer, and the Brooks sisters, among many others. These women found the freedom to strike out on their own in a fairly liberal religious era when conservative religious beliefs were already being reconsidered. The late nineteenth century saw the rise of liberal Christianities and a transcendentalism that countered the more conservative views of the time. In addition, these women were afforded some latitude because the movements in which they were active were considered marginal religions. For example, Mary Baker Eddy was considered to be a bit of a hysterical woman because of her various ailments and her sermons on "malicious magnetism." She was perceived to be so un-orthodox as to pose no real threat to such firmly en-trenched churches as the Congregationalists and Presbyte-rians. Her teachings did not threaten to overthrow the Christian mainstays, so her leadership was not considered a threat.

Today as well, New Thought religions are still considered marginal, particularly among African Americans, and the teachings are still unorthodox compared to mainstream Christianity. The female leadership in these religions is negligible compared to the stronghold of African American men in Christian ministry. Thus, the women in New Thought, though numerous, are not considered to be com-petition for Christian pulpits. It is noteworthy that the Black Christian megachurches that are incorporating New Thought principles continue to be led by men, and it will be interesting to see if that tradition persists as the new doctrine continues to be absorbed.

Female leadership in New Thought churches remains the norm because the historical legacy of important women could not very easily be controverted. However, even at East Bay Church of Religious Science some of the congregants have raised it for discussion. Some people at first expressed surprise or discomfort with a female pastor. For example, one former Baptist shared that he found Rev. E's messages to be "eloquent and relevant," yet initially he felt "apprehensive about female leadership, but I allowed myself to attend through the recognition of the African heritage where women are honored."[4] Another person commented: "East Bay is the first church I ever attended with a woman pastor. I never saw that in the Episcopal church, and of course not in the Catholic church that I also attended growing up."[5] One woman expressed her satisfaction with Rev. E as follows: "I can really relate to her as a Black woman and I respect her as an older Black woman."[6]

As New Thought teachings and churches continue to gain prominence among African Americans, as I believe they will, it will be interesting to see if the traditional criticism against female pastors will be an issue. Will women be seen as competitors for church members and therefore be perceived as a threat to the male-dominated ministry? Or will female leadership help promote New Thought as a marginal religion?

Another question I raise is whether this religious philosophy serves as a critique or reflection of American society. Through the specific lens of African American followers of New Thought, I ask how this philosophy might mirror or stand apart from the larger socioeconomic picture. Implied within the New Thought belief system is an ardent resistance to the idea that circumstances such as poverty and discrimination necessarily prohibit an individual from achieving success. What I have found among the African Americans I interviewed is that adherence to New Thought beliefs reflects their desire to participate more fully in the social and economic opportunities that surround them in the larger culture. Inspired by religious faith, these believers see the world as a prosperous place and take an active role in obtaining their own piece of it. Instead of standing apart from the larger social order, followers of New Thought seek to benefit within it. New Thought is a "despite all appearances" type of philosophy in which followers are encouraged to succeed, even against the odds. This phenomenon implies consent with the social and economic systems of the larger American society. Thus any implied criticism I have observed is not directed against the social or economic systems themselves, but against the standard societal norm that expects success for only well-educated and well-connected people, usually excluding people of color or the poor, though entertainers and athletes are often accepted as exceptions to this rule. New Thought teachings do not shun societal emphasis on material success; on the contrary, they believe that success in all aspects of one's life is the natural order. The socioeconomic dimension of African Americans in New Thought is substantial enough to merit a study of its own. I raise it here as a point that should be more adequately fleshed out in future scholarship.

Alongside these discussions, the phenomenon of African Americans who follow New Thought religion leads to implications that religion scholars should bear in mind. For example, the narrowly focused ideas about what constitutes legitimate religious practice for African Americans must be reconsidered. While traditional scholarship in African American religious studies has focused on Christianity as the normative religious expression for African Americans, this project has expanded this narrow view by examining why African Americans participate in New Thought religions. The expansion of New Thought shows that African Americans continue to practice multiple forms of religious expressions as they always have. The religious beliefs and practices of African Americans should be understood to be plural and the scholarship should reflect diverse expressions. Though scholars may be aware of the plurality of African American community activities and religious expressions, the formal discourse has not been sufficiently inclusive to extend legitimacy to that plurality.

At the East Bay Church of Religious Science, I have been able to observe a community of African Americans who have reappropriated a "foreign" religion according to their own sensibilities and needs. Members of this community observe social intersections that have led them away from

the conventional teachings of their previous religious affiliations. I have learned that this community moves beyond
restrictive categories of ontological authenticity by defer-
ring to their belief system that says all is one. Matters of difference are not judged good or bad, authentic or inauthentic; particularity is believed to be part of the universal oneness. The diverse social locations that people at this church
occupy are not believed to compromise racial authenticity.
On the contrary, the comments I have heard reflect their
comfort with their religious beliefs and practices while they
are also maintaining their cultural connections. The community runs counter to the larger African American society
that seeks to gauge the authenticity of its members depend-
ing on where individuals fall in matters of class, politics, religion, sexuality, and so on. They are an African American
community whose members share cultural memories such
as dehumanizing oppression, but they are positively re-visioning themselves via their religious consciousness.
African Americans are still adapting alternative religious
practices such as New Thought for their own use. Churches
such as the East Bay Church of Religious Science are an indication that New Thought teachings and denominations
are making an impact on the ways in which African Americans think about religion.

History in the Making: Contemporary African American New Thought Leaders and Practices

In addition to some Christian appropriation of New
Thought teachings, and despite resistance from some
mainstream Christian institutions, the presence of African
Americans in the broader spectrum of New Thought religions is expanding. Contrary to John Simmons and Brian

Wilson's position that New Thought churches are dwindling in number due to the aging of their congregations and to advances in healthcare that have diminished reliance on prayer and religion for healing, I maintain that New Thought teachings are expanding through the growth of independent Black New Thought churches and the continued growth of megachurches such as the Word of Faith ministries.[7]

Many churches and personalities, both independent and denominationally affiliated, are sprouting as focal points of African American religious leadership. In addition to Rev. Ike, one of the earliest African American New Thought personalities, is Rev. Dr. Johnnie Colemon, who established an active New Thought congregation as early as 1956. As we saw, Rev. Colemon is the founder of the Universal Foundation for Better Living (UFBL) in Chicago, an international organization that currently is comprised of thirty-three member churches and study groups. She began her career in the Unity tradition and even served as the first African American president of the Association of Unity Churches. She discontinued her association with them in 1974 due to a number of incidences of racism. Her own church, Christ Unity Temple, was then established as an independent New Thought church. The church affirms this belief:

> Every individual on the face of this earth should live a happy, healthy, prosperous life. The nature of God is absolute Good, and God cannot give anything but Himself which is Good. We believe that the UFBL is a Vehicle for which these principles are to be expressed.[8]

Rev. Colemon currently serves as President Emeritus of the UFBL organization, which is also a member of the International New Thought Alliance (INTA). She has served as a mentor and leader for many African Americans in New Thought, particularly African American women. A look at the affiliated church list shows that only one is not led by a woman.[9] Interestingly, the list also includes a church in Los Angeles headed by the well-known actress, Della Reese. The UFBL is currently under the primary leadership of the Reverend Mary Tumpkin, who is also senior minister of her own member church in Miami, Florida. Rev. Mary, as she is known, started the Universal Truth Center in 1982 with a congregation of 130. According to church literature, the empowering New Thought message was positively accepted in the Miami community, and the church grew quickly, requiring larger space in 1983, 1985, and 1993. Since its last move in 1993, the Universal Truth Center has occupied a 22,000-square-foot facility. The mission statement of the church is "to empower people to develop their potential by awakening their Divine nature."[10]

Another prominent African American New Thought leader is Dr. Barbara King, founder and senior minister of Atlanta's Hillside Chapel and Truth Center, Inc. Dr. King started the Hillside Chapel and Truth Center in 1971 as a nondenominational, ecumenical ministry. Hillside emphasizes the divine potential within every child of God and teaches that, through practical understanding and application of what Jesus taught, every person can realize and express his or her divine potential for a happier, fuller, and more successful life.[11]

This church has grown to have significant respect and influence in Atlanta, and Dr. King has often been recognized for her contributions to the community. The local newspaper, the *Atlanta Journal-Constitution*, has described her as "legendary for her ministry in Atlanta."[12] In addition, she has won numerous honors, including being named by the Atlanta Business League as one of "Atlanta's

Top 100 Black Women of Influence" in 2000.[13] On the national scene, Dr. King was recognized as a community
leader by the leading African American women's magazine
Essence as an honoree at their annual Essence Awards in
1987.[14]

Under the leadership of Rev. Dr. Michael Beckwith,
Agape International Spiritual Center, which I mentioned
earlier, was founded as a multicultural, transdenomina-
tional spiritual community in 1985 in Rev. Beckwith's own
home. The church has swelled to seven thousand members
since then, and now holds two services each Sunday in the
Culver City neighborhood of Los Angeles. As a Religious
Science church, the teachings of Ernest Holmes are supported with biblical text. A *USA Today* article reports that
"familiar hymns and gospel rhythms weave through several
songs, and snippets of Scripture float through Beckwith's
sermons."[15]

Rev. Beckwith has developed something of a celebrity
profile himself. He holds many service positions in the Los
Angeles community, the United Church of Religious Science organization, and the larger Global New Thought association. His community awards are numerous, including
a Humanitarian Award and the Martin Luther King, Jr.,
Peace Award.[16] The church has received much recognition
both because of Rev. Beckwith's leadership, and because of
the many celebrities who attend. The church will be
filmed as part of a British documentary on spirituality in
Los Angeles, and Rev. Beckwith has recently met with the
Dalai Lama at an international conference on New
Thought in Italy. Finally, Agape Church of Religious Science and East Bay Church of Religious Science are in regular fellowship with one another. Rev. Beckwith and Rev.
Elouise Oliver are both personal friends and professional
colleagues.

Finally, an African American who has had perhaps the greatest reach for the New Thought message in contemporary history is Iyanla Vanzant, acclaimed author, former talk show hostess, Yoruba priestess, and founder of a Maryland-based spiritual center, Inner Visions Worldwide. Her body of work includes *Tapping the Power Within: A Path to Self-Empowerment for Black Women*, a guidebook that emphasizes the empowerment principles of Yoruba; two daily affirmation books, *Acts of Faith* and *Until Today*; *In the Meantime*, a book for helping readers make sense of crisis points in their lives; a companion workbook to *In the Meantime* called *Living through the Meantime*, in which readers can document their own experiences and progress in the form of a journal; and the textbook-style volume *One Day My Soul Just Opened Up: 40 Days and 40 Nights towards Spiritual Strength and Personal Growth*. Her latest work, *Every Day I Pray: Prayers for Awakening to the Grace of Inner Communion*, is a daily prayer guide. In all of her books Vanzant is honest about her own challenges, past and present. Her success motivates people to move from lives of dissatisfaction to lives of conscious choices. Her books are not passive; they provoke the reader to take positive action in his or her own life.

Although her power base is not a church pulpit, her message of personal empowerment, spirituality, and love is shaped by her Unity–New Thought religious orientation, as she writes in one of her books:

I had learned to combine the universal Principles I was learning through Unity with the cultural principles I had learned in Yoruba. . . . It was the teachings of Unity, [The] Course in Miracles, and a metaphysical understanding of the Bible that helped me to build Iyanla's character.[17]

Through her books, television appearances on *Oprah,* and her own short-lived syndicated show, *Iyanla,* she has managed to bring this message into mainstream conversations and churches. The range of her supporters is evidence that her spiritual leadership is being accepted among African Americans. Like Dr. Barbara King, Vanzant's leadership role has been recognized by *Essence* magazine. She currently has a monthly advice column with the magazine, and she has been the subject of several articles over the years.[18] In addition, she was a panelist at a February 2002 summit discussion on "Where Do We Go from Here? A Forum on African-American Issues since September 11." The program was held at Sharon Baptist Church in Philadelphia and televised by the C-span network. It was billed as an African American "think tank" by its organizers, noted journalists and radio talk show personalities Tavis Smiley and Tom Joyner. Their presence on the panel, shared with Barbara King, among others, represents a communal embrace of their particular wisdom and leadership. Vanzant's dynamic personality is helping to create a space on the spiritual landscape for the acceptance of New Thought religious teachings at a time when they are becoming increasingly visible in many African American communities.

Vanzant is reaching people from a variety of religious backgrounds. From interviews conducted with two of her staff members I learned that her supporters are a demographically diverse group, transcending racial differences; they represent all walks of life, the poor, the middle class and the wealthy, the young and the old.[19] Her supporters are generally people who want to maintain a sense of spirituality in their lives but may have rejected the formal doctrines of religion as inadequate and/or unfulfilling. They are seekers who desire an immanent connection to God.

They seek meaningful lives, learning to free themselves from unconscious, monotonous living, ineffective behavior patterns, and unsatisfying interpersonal relationships. Vanzant empowers them to heal old wounds that may be interfering with their growth and sabotaging their lives. They seem to share the desire to improve their circumstances and the willingness to be active in their own success. They are dissatisfied enough to try different tools and a new religious philosophy. I believe that people find Vanzant's message immanently practical. Her presentation style is a down-to-earth, grassroots approach that gives people important tools to transform their own lives.

Conclusions and Questions for Further Consideration

In this section I reflect upon a couple of the lingering thoughts and questions that I still have after my participant-observation with the East Bay Church of Religious Science community. The first is an inquiry into the possible implications of a church community that exhibits a lenient code of personal conduct or piety among churchgoers.

We have seen that Religious Science does not teach a doctrine of sin in the sense that any deed could separate a person from God, nor do members believe in a God who condemns people based on their actions. Rather, they affirm that human beings are free to do whatever they will, knowing that universal law will act impersonally and karmically return every action with a corresponding consequence. Since Religious Science offers no doctrinal moral code to its followers other than the all-encompassing directive to love one another, the community does not condemn others for their personal actions. I have often heard Rev. E direct the congregation to remove judgment from events that appear to be wrong or from people who seem to be misguided. Instead, she says, it is important to recognize that each person is always doing the best that he or she can at that moment, and that punitive judgments will not help, anyway.

I began to question the significance of the lax moral doctrine of Religious Science, more specifically to the membership of East Bay Church of Religious Science. I frequently heard from churchgoers that they appreciated East Bay Church for the individual freedom they felt, the nonjudgmental environment, and the total acceptance they received. This suggested to me that some members of the community may equate the accepting environment of EBCRS as permissive, one in which they feel particularly liberated from conventional social mores. This does not seem to have presented any outward problems for the church. I have not found any documentation within the church literature to suggest that immoral or inappropriate behavior had ever been corporately addressed as a problem. Incidents that may happen at the local church level are likely to be dealt with locally, and information on such events would become known only if people are willing to discuss them in a meaningful way. Assessments based on church gossip would not be fair or entirely accurate for a study like this one.

The second question of interest is, what makes this church attractive to the small number of non-Black people who regularly attend? My focus throughout the project has been to articulate why African Americans come to the church and why they remain, but a good line of questioning could also be pursued by investigating the fact that the church has a small nucleus of White, Asian, and Hispanic members who choose to worship in an environment that embodies a predominantly African American culture.

While I did not make these members part of my study, I observed their attendance as congregants and their participation in areas such as the choir and Practitioner corps, and as class facilitators.

Given the history of racial discrimination and religious segregation in the United States, I believe it is significant when members of different races manage to come together in worship. While integration is usually held up as an ideal, it has not shown itself to be the norm at Sunday morning worship services. Racial separation is still apparent in many denominations. There are White First Baptists and Black Second and Third Baptists, White Assemblies of God Pentecostals and Black Church of God in Christ Pentecostals, and White United Methodists and Black AME, AMEZ, and CME Methodists.

When considering the small cultural mix at East Bay Church of Religious Science, the argument could be made that the makeup of the church reflects to some degree the population of the larger Bay Area, which consists largely of Asian/Pacific Islanders, Hispanics, Whites, and Blacks.[20] Still, there are other Religious Science churches throughout the area. What is it about EBCRS that has a cross-cultural appeal? Further, what insights could be gained from these individuals for the advancement of race relations? These are questions for a separate study.

The focus of this book has been to feature the East Bay Church of Religious Science in order to gain a better understanding of New Thought religious phenomena. In addition, we have explored the larger issue of African American religious diversity in an attempt to urge academic and theological discourse to include a broader range of religious phenomena. I have shown that New Thought fits into the landscape of African American religious life so much that it is influencing the way the concept of "African American religion" is defined and discussed. As I have maintained, African American religious studies have traditionally been narrowly construed to focus on Christian theology and an occasional nod to Islam; now, the presence of New Thought churches within African American communities is witness to the necessity of broadening the study of African American religions. Scholarly accounts of these religions that do not recognize the influence of New Thought figures such as Johnnie Colemon, Barbara King, and Iyanla Vanzant fail to give a full representation of the actual religious practices of African Americans. The East Bay Church of Religious Science is helping to usher New Thought ideas into mainstream Christian churches and into the conversations of people at a grassroots level.

Appendix

Ten Core Concepts of the
United Church of Religious Science[1]

There is one cosmic reality principle and presence in the universe—God. All creation originates in this one Source. God is. God is all there is.

God is triune, or threefold, in nature, having three aspects or modes of Being within the One: Spirit, Soul and Body. This is God as macrocosm.

Spirit is the great Causative Power of the Universe. The Word, or thought, of God eternally initiates the Divine Creative Process. In this process, Law is continuously set in motion to create, from the Unformed Substance, innumerable forms which follow the thought patterns of Spirit.

In the Infinite Nature of God, all conceivable Good is eternally available, ready to flow into human experience. Through some Cosmic Process, this flow of Good is activated and/or increased by human belief, faith, and acceptance. The expression of this essential belief, faith, and acceptance is prayer.

This is a Universe of Wholeness, Allness, Oneness. Spirit is a transcendent, perfect Whole that, in its Infinite inclusivity, harmoniously embraces all *seeming* opposites.

This is a Universe of infinite abundance, spiritual, mental and physical. This bounty of Spirit, this Allness of Good, is limitless and can never be exhausted or depleted.

This is a reciprocal Universe. For every visible form, there is an invisible counterpart. Everything in nature tends to equalize itself, to keep its balance true.

The Universe exists in the Eternal Now, each moment complete and perfect within itself. In this Universal Harmony, justice without judgment is always automatic, an infallible Universal Principle. There can be no place for Divine anger, unforgiveness, or punishment.

Immortality is a Universal Principle, not a "belief" or a bargain made with the Universe for good behavior. God knows only Life, its eternal continuity, evolution, and expansion.

The mystic concept of the Cosmic Christ is not that of a person, but of a Principle, a Universal Presence . . . the Universal Image of God present in all creation . . . the "pattern that connects."

Sequence and Scope of Certified Classes (taken from a church informational flyer)

Scope of Classes:

Classes listed below comprise the certified education classes offered by the United Church of Religious Science. The student who completes the foundational and other Spiritual Development Classes will have a comprehensive understanding of the Core Concepts of Science of Mind.

She or he will be able to do Spiritual Mind Treatment for self and others, and will know where our principles come from, and will have explored healing and consciousness.

Certified classes are divided into five branches of learning:

prerequisite courses
Foundational (45 hours)
Spiritual Practices for Daily Living (35 hours)

history/philosophy courses
Roots 2003 (45 hours)
Edinburgh Lectures (24 hours)
Bible Wisdom (30–45 hours)

consciousness courses
Practical Mysticism (30 hours)
The Mind/Body Connection (24 hours)

practical application
Financial Freedom (24 hours)
Principles of Successful Living (24 hours)
Self-Mastery (24 hours)

professional studies
Professional Practitioner I (90 hours)
Professional Practitioner II (90 hours)
Ministerial Education through Holmes Institute (3 to 5 years)

Sequence:

Once the Foundational and Spiritual Practices classes have been taken, other classes can be taken in any order. It is highly recommended that classes are *not taken concurrently.*

After taking the Foundational and Spiritual Practices classes, students interested in continuing into Professional Studies choose two courses from either History/Philosophy, Consciousness or Practical Application Branches.

New Thought Websites

African American New Thought Churches and Organizations

The official Website for the East Bay Church of Religious Science: http://www.ebcrs.org.

The official Website for Christ Universal Temple in Chicago, Illinois, founded by Dr. Johnnie Colemon: http://www.cutemplelife.org.

The Universal Foundation for Better Living is the organization founded by Dr. Colemon. This umbrella organization consists of a number of African-American New Thought churches: http://www.ufbl.org.

The official Website for the Hillside Chapel and Truth Center, pastored by Dr. Barbara King: http://www.Hillsidechapel.org.

The official Website for Agape International Spiritual Center, a religious science church, pastored by Dr. Michael Beckwith: http://www.agapelive.com.

General New Thought Websites

The official Website of the United Church of Religious Science: http://www.ReligiousScience.org.

The official Website of Religious Science International: http://www.rsintl.org.

The New Thought Movement Homepage, which contains a spattering of New Thought teachings across the board. It is a good site for linking to the world of various New Thought religions: www.websyte.com/alan.

The Website for the affiliated New Thought network, an organization of independent Religious Science ministries: www.Newthought.org.

The official Website of the Association for Global New Thought: http://www.agnt.org.

The official Website of the Unity School of Christianity: http://www.agnt.org.

New Thought Broadcasting, an online community where members may listen to audio clips and view video clips of New Thought messages from recognized leaders: http://www.newthoughtbroadcasting.com.

Notes

NOTES TO THE INTRODUCTION

1. Joachim Wach, "The Meaning and Task of the History of Religions," *Introduction to the History of Religions*, ed. Joseph Kitagawa and Gregory Alles (New York: Macmillan, 1988).

2. James P. Spradley, *Participant Observation* (Fort Worth, TX: Harcourt Brace, 1980) 10.

3. Ibid. 13.

4. These steps are specified as part of the participant-observation technique by the scholarly team of the *Ethnographer's Toolkit*, vol. 2, 91.

5. Robert M. Emerson, Rachel I. Fretz, et al. *Writing Ethnographic Fieldnotes* (Chicago: University of Chicago Press, 1995) 179–181.

NOTES TO CHAPTER 1

1. Ernest Holmes, *Religious Science Foundational Class Manual* (Los Angeles: United Church of Religious Science) 1.7, 1992.

2. Ibid.

3. Ernest Holmes, *Living the Science of Mind* (Marina del Rey, CA: DeVorss, 1984) 69.

4. Ibid. 18.

5. Matthew 8:13, NRSV.

6. Martin A. Larson makes a strong case for the primary authority of Emanuel Swedenborg as "the grand fountainhead of a variety of deviationist religious movements, and, specifically, the grandfather of New Thought." *New Thought Religion: A Philosophy for Health, Happiness, and Prosperity* (New York: Philosophical Library, 1987) 9. Additionally, Gail Harley challenges this position in light of the reevaluation of the influence and legacy of Emma Curtis Hopkins. Harley, *Emma Curtis Hopkins: Forgotten Founder of New Thought* (Syracuse, NY: Syracuse University Press, 2002).

7. P. P. Quimby, *The Complete Writings,* ed. Ervin Seale, 3 vols. (Marina del Rey, CA: DeVorss, 1988) 3:26, 3:210.

8. P. P. Quimby, *The Quimby Manuscripts,* ed. Horatio W. Dresser (Secaucus, NJ: Citadel Press, 1961) 185–186.

9. Evans was known for his work as a great systematizer. His writings included *Mental Medicine* (1872), *Soul and Body* (1875), and his most widely known work, *The Divine Law of Cure* (1881). Mary Baker Eddy went on to found the First Church of Christ, Scientist. The Dressers were considered the keepers of Quimby's legacy as teachers in Boston, and later their son Horatio Dresser edited Quimby's long-awaited manuscript.

10. Quimby, *Quimby Manuscripts,* Appendix I.433.

11. Charles S. Braden, *Spirits in Rebellion: The Rise and Development of New Thought* (Dallas: Southern Methodist University Press, 1963) 143.

12. Harley, *Emma Curtis Hopkins,* and Ferne Anderson, "Emma Curtis Hopkins: Springboard to New Thought," M.A. thesis, University of Denver, 1981.

13. By 1886 Hopkins had established her own teaching center in Chicago, which still revolved around the tenets she had learned from Mary Baker Eddy. She taught extensively in many cities and eventually founded the Christian Science Theological Seminary in Chicago in 1887. By the time Hopkins's ministry had come to an end at her death in 1925, she had established a seminary, written numerous articles and two books, instituted an eponymous association that hosted annual meetings for her many students and adherents, popularized a new biblical hermeneutic, and inspired a legion of followers who would continue and expand her work after her death.

14. Harley, *Emma Curtis Hopkins* 20–21.

15. This group started as a result of an effort to bring together growing numbers of mental science leaders, and would eventually grow into the present umbrella organization, the International New Thought Alliance (INTA).

16. Divine Science was founded by Malinda Cramer of San Francisco and Nona Brooks and Fannie Brooks (James) of Colorado. They established the Divine Science College in 1898 and the First Divine Science Church in Denver in 1899. Unity was founded by Charles and Myrtle Fillmore as a result of their own personal healings. They started the Unity School of Christianity in Kansas City in 1889 after coming into contact with the teachings of Emma Curtis Hopkins in 1886.

17. Fenwick Holmes, *Ernest Holmes: His Life and Times* (New York: Dodd, Mead, 1970) 87.

18. Ibid. 117.
19. Ibid. 149.
20. See Appendix for a listing of all ten core concepts.
21. Holmes, *Science of Mind* 307.
22. Rev. E's lecture, Foundations Class, October 17, 2000.
23. Holmes, *Science of Mind* 18.
24. Class Manual 2.6.
25. Ibid. 3.5.
26. Ibid.
27. Holmes, *Science of Mind* 289.
28. Class Manual 4.9.
29. Ibid.
30. "Augustine," *Encyclopedia of Early Christianity*, 2nd ed., ed. Everett Ferguson, Michael P. McHugh, et al. (New York: Garland, 1990) 837–840.
31. Class Manual 7.5.
32. Ibid. 7.11
33. Holmes, *Science of Mind* 253.
34. Class Manual 9.1–9.2.
35. Foundations Class, October 17, November 7, 2000.
36. Holmes, *Science of Mind*, 397.
37. Ibid. 83–104.

NOTES TO CHAPTER 2

1. "The Blessing Factor," *Abundant Life Cathedral Ministries*, Black Entertainment Television, July 26, 2002.

2. The history of African American plantation religion has been well rehearsed, so I simply refer the reader to classic texts such as *Slave Religion* by Albert Raboteau; *African-American Religious History: A Documentary Witness* by Milton Sernett, and *Black Religion* by Joseph Washington. For discussions of non-Christian slave religions, see also Sylviane A. Diouf, who notes that the most common alternative religious practices among the enslaved Africans were Islam and variations of African traditional religions. In *Servants of Allah: African Muslims Enslaved in the Americas* (New York: NYU Press, 1998), she argues that West African Muslims did not succumb to acculturation but strove hard to maintain their traditions, social values, customs, and particular identity.

3. Gayraud Wilmore, *Black Religion and Black Radicalism* (Garden City, NY: Doubleday, 1972) 36–39.

4. Joseph R. Washington, Jr., *Black Religion: The Negro and Christianity in the United States* (Boston: Beacon Press, 1964) 202.

5. Schism within each of these denominations has led to the development of different bodies, hence there are seven organizations that are typically regarded as representing African American church life: the African Methodist Episcopal Church (AME); the African Methodist Episcopal Zion Church (AMEZ); the Christian, formerly Colored, Methodist Church (CME); the National Baptist Convention, U.S.A., Incorporated (NBC); the National Baptist Convention of America, Unincorporated (NBCA); the Progressive National Baptist Convention (PNBC); and the Church of God in Christ (COGIC).

6. C. Eric Lincoln and Lawrence H. Mamiya, *The Black Church in the African-American Experience* (Durham, NC: Duke University Press, 1990) 1.

7. While patterns of Black migrations to California came principally from Texas, Arkansas, and Louisiana, other identifiable patterns note Blacks moving from the Southeast (Florida to Virginia) to Pennsylvania, the mid-Atlantic states, and New England; and Blacks in Detroit and Chicago often migrating from Kentucky, Tennessee, Alabama, and Mississippi. See Blyden Jackson, "Introduction: A Street of Dreams," in *Black Exodus: The Great Migration from the American South,* ed. Alferdteen Harrison (Jackson: University Press of Mississippi, 1991) xvii.

8. Fauset uses this term to refer to religious cult phenomena occurring in northern urban cities. See his work, *Black Gods of the Metropolis* (Philadelphia: University of Pennsylvania Press, 1944).

9. Nonmainstream religions are often designated as cults or sects, terms that can have a derogatory connotation. For a discussion of these terms and their more accurate meanings, see Rodney Stark and William Bainbridge, *The Future of Religion: Secularization, Revival and Cult Formation* (Berkeley: University of California Press, 1985); Hans Baer and Merrill Singer, *African-American Religion in the Twentieth Century: Varieties of Protest and Accommodation* (Knoxville: University of Tennessee Press, 1992); and Joseph Washington, *Black Sects and Cults* (Garden City, NY: Doubleday, 1972).

10. Baer and Singer, *African-American Religion* 179–213.

11. Ibid. 179–180.

12. Ibid. 179.

13. A significant difference is the use of the word "spiritual" by Black groups instead of "spiritualism," the latter implying a perceived emphasis on seances and fortune-telling, and the former defined as a recognition of God's spiritual nature that naturally results in a spiritual worship relationship and lifestyle. See Baer, *The Black Spiritual Move-*

ment: A Religious Response to Racism (Knoxville: University of Tennessee Press 1984) 115.

14. Ibid.

15. Ibid. 160–169.

16. This varies somewhat from the spiritualist tradition in New Orleans, which more commonly centers around the veneration of a community of saints. In this respect, elements of Catholicism and African American and Afro-Caribbean religions such as Vodun, Candomble, and Santeria are more prominent.

17. Baer, *Black Spiritual Movement* 191.

18. Recall the movements led by "Dr." P. P. Quimby, Mary Baker Eddy, Emma Curtis Hopkins, and Myrtle and Charles Fillmore, among others.

19. Sara Harris, *Father Divine* (New York: Collier, 1971) 128.

20. *Father Divine Peace Mission Home Page*, March 31, 2002. http://www.libertynet.org/fdipmm/.

21. *Reverend Ike Home Page*, March 31, 2002. http://www.revike.org/revike/whoike.asp/.

22. Martin Gallatin, "Rev. Ike's Ministry: A Sociological Investigation of Religious Innovation," Ph.D. diss., New York University, 1979, 194–209.

23. *Reverend Ike Homepage.*

24. Washington, *Black Sects and Cults* 115; noted as well by the *Reverend Ike Homepage.*

25. Religious Movements Homepage: Charles "Sweet Daddy" Grace and the United House of Prayer for All People, April 19, 2001; University of Virginia, April 6, 2002. http://www.religiousmovements.lib.virginia.edu/nrms/daddy_grace.html#10t.

26. Fauset, *Black Gods* 26.

27. Ibid. 30.

28. "The Doctrines of the Church of God in Christ: The Holy Ghost," December 20, 2001. http://www.cogic.org/doctrine.htm.

29. Ernest Holmes, *Living the Science of Mind* (Marina del Rey, CA: DeVorss, 1984) 83–104.

30. Raymond J. Cunningham, "From Holiness to Healing: The Faith Cure in America 1872–1892," *Church History* 43.3 (1974): 507–508.

31. The Bible, James 5:14–15, and Mark 16:15–18.

32. "The Doctrines of the Church of God in Christ: Divine Healing," December 20, 2001. http://www.cogic.org/doctrine.htm.

33. Malinda Cramer, Charles and Myrtle Fillmore, and Mary Baker Eddy each reported their experiences of personal healings in their respective literature.

34. Holmes, *Science of Mind* 83–104.
35. *Ever Increasing Word Ministries Homepage,* March 19, 2003. http://www.eiwm.org.
36. Ibid. http://www.faithdome.org.
37. *Ever Increasing Word Ministries Homepage.*
38. "Creflo Dollar Ministries," *World Changers Church International,* Black Entertainment Television, March 16, 2003.
39. "The Blessing Factor," *Abundant Life Cathedral Ministries,* Black Entertainment Television, July 26, 2002.
40. *Abundant Life Cathedral Homepage,* March 19, 2003. http://www.abundantlifecathedral.org/montgomery.
41. "Creflo Dollar Ministries," *World Changers Church International,* Black Entertainment Television, November 30, 2003.
42. "U-Win," *Abundant Life Cathedral,* Black Entertainment Network, February 16, 2001.
43. Interview, September 2002.
44. Interview, September 2002.
45. Interview, August 2002.
46. Interview, December 2002.

NOTES TO CHAPTER 3

1. Delores Nason McBroome, *Parallel Communities: African-Americans in California's East Bay 1850–1963* (New York: Garland, 1993) 65.
2. John Simmons and Brian Wilson. *Competing Visions of Paradise: The California Experience of Nineteenth-Century American Sectarianism* (Santa Barbara: Fithian Press, 1993) 19, 70–71.
3. See ibid. for a brief exploration of religions finding a home in California, including the Mormons, Adventists, Christian Scientists, New Thought followers, and Pentecostals.
4. Interview, November 2003.
5. Interview, November 2002.
6. Interview, September 2002.
7. Suzanne Stewart, Mary Praerzellis, et al., eds., *Sights and Sounds: Essays in Celebration of West Oakland* (Rohnert Park, CA: Sonoma State University Academic Foundation, 1997); see also *Oakland Independent,* October 19, 1929, 8.
8. Chauncey Bailey, "African-American Roots," *Oakland Tribune,* February 7, 2002, L6.
9. Ibid. Bailey quotes veteran Black journalist Thomas Fleming, who at age ninety-seven was still writing for the *Sun Reporter.*
10. McBroome, *Parallel Communities* 65.

11. Ibid. 67.

12. This historical event was dramatized by the Showtime cable television network in the film *10,000 Men Named George,* shown in February and March 2002. It documents the twelve-year struggle of Black Pullman porters against the Pullman Car Company, from 1925 to 1937.

13. James A. Noel, "The Search for Zion," Ph.D. diss., Graduate Theological Union, 1999, 39.

14. Marilyn Johnson, *The Second Gold Rush: Oakland and the East Bay in World War II* (Berkeley: University of California Press, 1993) 6–8.

15. Vivian Bowie interview, "West Oakland Oral History Interviews," conducted by Bill Jersey and Marjorie Dobkin for the documentary film *Crossroads: A Story of West Oakland* (1995) 212–216.

16. Landon Williams interview, "West Oakland Oral History Interviews," 1994, 256–257.

17. Douglas Henry Daniels, *Pioneer Urbanites* (Berkeley: University of California Press, 1990) 18.

18. For a presentation of discriminatory housing procedures in the greater Bay Area, see Noel's "Search for Zion" for a discussion of the plight of African Americans in Marin City, California, in the post–World War II era.

19. Ferenc Morton Szasz, *Religion in the Modern American West* (Tucson: University of Arizona Press, 2000) 172. Also, Albert S. Broussard, *Black San Francisco* (Lawrence: University Press of Kansas, 1993) 183–184.

20. Gayraud S. Wilmore, "Doing the Truth: Some Criteria for Researching African-American Religious History," in *African-American Religion: Research Problems and Resources for the 1990s* (New York: Schomberg Center for Research in Black Culture, 1992) 136.

21. Dona L. Irvin offers significant original research of an Oakland church as well in her book, *The Unsung Heart of Black America: A Middle Class Church at Mid-Century* (Columbia: University of Missouri Press, 1992). In that work she chronicles the history and the experiences of forty members of Downs Memorial United Methodist Church during the 1950s and 1960s.

22. Interview, August 2001.

23. Interview, August 2001.

24. Interview, August 22, 2001. Pseudonym used.

25. The Panthers listed specific urban projects as the culprits in the disintegration of West Oakland as a community: BART, the Acorn Housing Project, the new freeways, the new Post Office, and the closing

of public housing. See Robert Owen Self, "Shifting Ground in Metropolitan America: Class, Race and Power in Oakland and the East Bay, 1945–1977," Ph.D. diss., University of Washington, 1998, for an analysis of the Oakland political environment during that period.

26. "This Far by Faith: African-American Spiritual Journeys," creator Henry Hampton, PBS, Episode 2, June 25, 2003.

NOTES TO CHAPTER 4

1. Interview, October 3, 2002.

2. Interview, October 8, 2002.

3. Interview, September 14, 2002.

4. Interview, September 5, 2002.

5. Interview, October 19, 2002.

6. Interview, October 18, 2002.

7. Interview, October 19, 2002.

8. Interview, August 30, 2002.

9. East Bay Church of Religious Science Mission Statement, taken from the Sunday program.

10. Martin G. Reynolds, "A Call to End Wave of Homicides: Clergy in Oakland Focus on Youths," *Oakland Tribune*, July 11, 2002.

11. Cecily Burt, Chauncey Bailey, and Martin G. Reynolds, "Community Acts to End the Killing: 4000 Vow to Take Back the Mean Streets," *Oakland Tribune*, July 14, 2002.

12. Reynolds, "A Call."

13. Ibid.

14. Personal interview with East Bay Church of Religious Science member, September 15, 2002.

15. Interview, September 14, 2002.

16. Sunday sermon, January 5, 2003.

17. Rev. E's class lecture, Science of Mind Foundations, November 7, 2000.

18. EBCRS Sunday service, October 6, 2002, and October 13, 2002.

19. RSI Information Packet, Religious Science International, Spokane, Washington, 1999.

20. United Church of Religious Science homepage: http://www.religiousscience.org/transition/cca.htm.

21. Personal interview, October 19, 2002.

22. Personal interview, October 4, 2002.

23. Personal interview, October 4, 2002.

24. EBCRS Sunday service, July 28, 2002

25. EBCRS Sunday service, November 14, 2001.

26. Personal interview, August 29, 2002.

27. Interview, August 29, 2002.

28. Depictions of Jesus as a Black man became prominent during the Black Power era of the 1960s and 1970s, and reflected the new "Black is Beautiful" cultural anthem.

29. Interview, August 29, 2002.

30. Interview, August 29, 2002.

31. Interview, August 29, 2002.

32. Interview, August 29, 2002.

33. Interview, August 29, 2002.

34. American Community Survey Profile: http://www.census.gov.

35. Melvin Williams, *Community in a Black Pentecostal Church* (Pittsburgh: University of Pittsburgh Press, 1974).

36. Ibid. 61–81.

37. Pseudonym.

38. Tucker interview.

39. Pseudonym.

40. Luke, conversation.

41. Pseudonym.

42. Williams, *Community* 76.

43. Both names are pseudonyms.

44. Smith, conversation.

45. Smith, conversation.

46. Interview, September 5, 2002.

47. Interview, October 4, 2002

48. Interview, October 8, 2002.

49. Interview, October 19, 2002.

50. Interview, November 27, 2002.

51. Interview, January 3, 2003.

52. Interview, September 5, 2002.

53. Interview, October 8, 2002.

54. Interview, September 15, 2002.

55. Interview, September 19, 2002.

56. This type of atypical event is known anthropologically as a critical event vignette and refers to an extreme, unique, or unusual event rather than the pattern. Scholars caution that focusing on such events can create a biased picture of the daily life of the community under study. See Stephen Schensul et al., *Ethnographer's Toolkit,* vol. 2 (Walnut Creek, CA: Altamira Press, 1999) 185.

57. Interview, November 15, 2002.

58. Interview, October 18, 2002.

59. Interview, October 19, 2002.

60. Interview, October 4, 2002.
61. September 6, 2002.
62. September 5, 2002.
63. December 7, 2002.
64. Sunday sermon, February 23, 2003.
65. Interview, September 19, 2002.

NOTES TO CHAPTER 5

1. Ernest Holmes, *Living the Science of Mind* (Marina del Rey, CA: DeVorss, 1984) 282.
2. Ibid. 499.
3. Ibid.
4. Ibid. 280.
5. Personal interview.
6. United Church of Religious Science, *Religious Science Foundational Class Manual* 1–7.
7. EBCRS Sunday sermon, January 5, 2003.
8. John 14:12.
9. Interview, January 3, 2003.
10. Interview, December 7, 2002.
11. Interview, October 19, 2002.
12. Holmes, *Science of Mind* 137–148.
13. Data gathered from public testimonials and private interviews.
14. Interview, September 14, 2002.
15. Holmes, *Science of Mind* 63–80.
16. Ibid. 266–378.
17. Hans Baer and Merrill Singer, *African-American Religion in the Twentieth Century: Varieties of Protest and Accommodation* (Knoxville: University of Tennessee Press, 1992) 57–64, 179–180.
18. Interview, November 27, 2002.
19. Interview, September 5, 2002.
20. Sunday sermon. This is a frequently repeated theme.
21. Schensul et al., *Ethnographer's Toolkit,* vol. 2.
22. EBCRS member, Foundations Class, December 2000.
23. EBCRS member, June 27, 2002.
24. Interview, October 2, 2002.
25. Inteview, December 21, 2002.
26. Interview, October 3, 2002.
27. Individual statements from eleven different interviews.
28. Interview, October 19, 2002.
29. Interview, October 4, 2002.

30. Interview, October 19, 2002.
31. Interview, November 15, 2002.
32. Interview, August 24, 2002.
33. Interview, August 30, 2002.
34. Interview, December 28, 2002.
35. Interview, November 27, 2002.
36. Interview, November 15, 2002.
37. Interview, November 27, 2002.
38. East Bay Church of Religious Science Newsletter, "Love in Action," August/September 2002; also, personal interview with minister, August 29, 2002.
39. J. Martin Favor, *Authentic Blackness: The Folk in the New Negro Renaissance* (Durham, NC: Duke University Press, 1999) 34.
40. C. E. Lincoln and L. Mamiya, *The Black Church in the African-American Experience* (Durham, NC: Duke University Press, 1990) 1–19.
41. Lincoln and Mamiya, *Black Church* 166.
42. James H. Evans, *We Have Been Believers: An African-American Systematic Theology* (Minneapolis: Fortress Press, 1992) 2.
43. Victor Anderson, *Beyond Ontological Blackness: An Essay on African-American Religious and Cultural Criticism* (New York: Continuum, 1995) 84.
44. Anderson quotes from Darlene Clark Hine's work, "In the Kingdom of Culture: Black Women and the Intersection of Race, Gender and Class," in *Lure and Loathing: Twenty Black Intellectuals Address W. E. B. Du Bois's Dilemma of the Double Consciousness of African-Americans,* ed. Gerald Early (New York: Penguin Group, 1993) 337–351.
45. Anderson, *Beyond Ontological Blackness* 87, 103–104, 112; Favor, *Authentic Blackness* 9, 13; bell hooks, *Yearnings: race, gender, and cultural politics* (Boston: South End Press, 1990) 19.
46. Michael Eric Dyson, *Reflecting Black: African-American Cultural Criticism* (Minneapolis: University of Minnesota Press, 1993) xviii. See also Cornel West, *Keeping Faith: Philosophy and Race in America* (New York: Routledge, 1993), and Toni Morrison, *Playing in the Dark: Whiteness and the Literary Imagination* (New York: Vintage Books, 1992).
47. Favor, *Authentic Blackness* 4.
48. Favor's essays highlight the literary works of James Weldon Johnson, Jean Toomer, Nella Larsen, and George S. Schuyler.
49. Favor, *Authentic Blackness* 21.
50. Anderson, *Beyond Ontological Blackness* 11.
51. Ibid. 144.
52. hooks, *Yearnings* 23–31.
53. Ibid. 15–22.

54. Quoted in Favor, *Authentic Blackness* 139. See also Trey Ellis, "The New Black Aesthetic," *Callaloo* 21, no. 1 (Winter 1989): 233–243.

55. Favor, *Authentic Blackness* 152.

56. Lincoln and Mamiya, *Black Church* 2, 7.

57. W. E. B. Du Bois, *The Souls of Black Folk* (New York: Penguin, 1995) 211.

58. Lincoln and Mamiya, *Black Church* 5.

59. Dwight N. Hopkins, *Black Theology of Liberation* (Maryknoll, NY: Orbis Books, 1999) 4–13; also see Theodore Walker, Jr., "A Black Neoclassical Social Ethics," in *Black Theology: A Documentary History,* vol. 2: *1980–1992,* ed. James H. Cone and Gayraud S. Wilmore (Maryknoll, NY: Orbis Books, 1993) 35–52.

60. Anthony B. Pinn, *Why Lord? Suffering and Evil in Black Theology* (New York: Continuum, 1995) 10, 17, 19.

61. See, for example, Roy D. Morrison II, "Self Transformation in American Blacks: The Harlem Renaissance and Black Theology," in *Existence in Black: An Anthology of Black Existential Philosophy,* ed. Lewis R. Gordon (New York: Routledge, 1997) 37–47.

NOTES TO CHAPTER 6

1. Community leaders such as Earl Graves, Tavis Smiley, and Randall Robinson have written and spoken on the necessity for economic empowerment as the next stage in the civil rights struggle. See the following references: Graves, "It's Not Over (Future of Affirmative Action)," *Black Enterprise,* July 2000; Smiley, *How to Make Black America Better: Leading African-Americans Speak Out* (New York: Doubleday, 2001); Randall Robinson, *The Debt: What America Owes to Blacks* (New York: Plume Publishing, 2001), and *The Reckoning: What Blacks Owe to Each Other* (New York: Dutton/Plume, 2002).

2. Gayraud Wilmore, *Black Religion and Black Radicalism* (Garden City, NY: Doubleday, 1972) 303.

3. Joseph R. Washington, Jr., *Black Religion: The Negro and Christianity in the United States* (Boston: Beacon Press, 1984) 38–39.

4. Interview, August 2002.

5. Interview, October 2002.

6. Interview, September 2002.

7. Simmons and Wilson affirm that New Thought groups and Christian Science are headed "the way of the dinosaur," unless they can accommodate other religious influences into their old messages and renew their followings. See *Competing Visions of Paradise* (Santa Barbara, CA: Fithian Press, 1993) 83–85.

8. S. DuPree, *African American Holiness Pentecostal Movement: An Annotated Bibliography* (New York: Garland, 1996) 379–380.

9. The Verity Center for Better Living of Toronto, Canada, is listed under the leadership of Rev. Evan Reid.

10. "Universal Truth Center: Who We Are," February 6, 2002. http://www.utruthcenter.org/utc_aboutus.html.

11. "What Is Hillside," April 27, 2002. http://207.150.221.91/ws-hillside/whatishillside.html.

12. Nadirah Z. Sabir, "Interfaith Groups Working Overtime," *Atlanta Journal-Constitution*, December 12, 2001.

13. "Atlanta Business League recognizes achievements of Families First's CEO," April 27, 2002. http://www.familiesfirst.org/news.html.

14. "2002 Essence Awards: Saluting Our Stars for Strengthening Our Communities," *Essence*, May 2002, 122.

15. Cathy Lynn Grossman, "Agape Gives Them 'New Thought' Religion," *USA Today*, November 5, 2001, Life section.

16. "Agape International Spiritual Center: Rev. Dr. Michael Beckwith," 2001 – 2002. http://www.agapelive.com/aboutagape/revdr-michaelbeckwith.html, April 27, 2002.

17. Iyanla Vanzant, *Yesterday, I Cried* (New York: Fireside, 1998), 247.

18. Cover story, *Essence*, August 2001, and the ongoing monthly advice column, "Ask Iyanla."

19. I conducted short interviews with two staff members from Inner Visions Spiritual Life Maintenance Network in Silver Springs, Maryland, in April 2002.

20. "Racial/Ethnic Diversity and Residential Segregation in the San Francisco Bay Area," No. 1, September 2001, Center for Comparative Studies in Race and Ethnicity (CCSRE), September 22, 2003. http://www.ccsre.stanford.edu/index.

NOTE TO THE APPENDIX

1. Foundational Class Manual (Los Angeles: United Church of Religious Science), rev. ed., 1993, A-4–A-13.

Index

Spiritualist: Black, 41–49, 42n13; and
New Thought, 45–49, 53; versus
spiritualism, 11, 37, 42; White, 43
Spradly, James, and ethnography, 6

Thompson, Leroy, 54
Troward, Thomas, 20
Tumpkin, Mary, 152

United Church of Religious Science,
23, 145; and East Bay Church of Religious Science, 84, 121

Unity School of Christianity: and
Black spiritualists, 46; and Iyanla
Vanzant, 154; and Johnnie Cole-
man, 151; Myrtle and Charles Fill-
more, 15, 17
Unitarianism: 37, 64

Vanzant, Iyanla, 154–156, 159

Washington, Joseph, 143
Williams, Melvin, 90–91, 95

About the Author

Darnise C. Martin earned her Ph.D. in Cultural and Historical Studies from the Graduate Theological Union in Berkeley, California, and her Master's in Theological Studies from the Methodist Theological School in Ohio. She has been a fellow of the Fund for Theological Education (FTE) for two years, and her research interests include varieties of African American religions, New Thought religions, and myth and religion.